# NARADA BHAKTI SUTRAS

# NARADA BHAKTI SUTRAS

## (REVISED EDITION)

### SRI SWAMI SIVANANDA

*Published By*

THE DIVINE LIFE SOCIETY
P.O. SHIVANANDANAGAR—249 192
Distt. Tehri-Garhwal, U.P., Himalayas, India

Price ]                    1998                    [ Rs. 50/-

First Edition:      1957
Second Edition:   1988
Third Edition:     1997

(3000 Copies)

ISBN   81-7052-068-1

Published by Swami Krishnananda for The Divine Life
Society, Shivanandanagar, and printed by him at the
Yoga-Vedanta forest Academy Press, P.O. Shivanandanagar,
Distt. Tehri-Garhwal, U.P., India

H.H. SWAMI SIVANANDAJI MAHARAJ

# PUBLISHERS' NOTE

According to the claim of a 'clairvoyant', Sri Swami Sivanandaji Maharaj is a re-incarnation of Sri Chaitanya Mahaprabhu, that supreme Bhakta who lived recently in Bengal. However that might be, it is undoubtedly true that after Mahaprabhu, it is Sri Swamiji Maharaj who gave the greatest impetus to Sankirtan Bhakti Yoga, who revived mass singing of the Maha Mantra and who exalted Bhakti as Sadhana equal to, if not better than, Vedantic Nididhyasana or Raja Yogic meditation.

Sri Swamiji's commentary on the Narada Bhakti Sutras, therefore, has in it the soul-force of a Para Bhakta who echoes the Word of God.

It is, therefore, hoped that this commentary on the Bhakti Sutras will inspire aspirants to practise Bhakti Yoga and reach the lotus -feet of the Lord.

—THE DIVINE LIFE SOCIETY

# INTRODUCTION

The Narada Bhakti Sutras is a very popular treatise in India on Bhakti Yoga.. This treatise is very lucid and practical in its exposition of the birth, growth, development, unfoldment and expression of Bhakti. This is a very useful book for earnest and sincere aspirants who tread the path of devotion.

This book is a great standard work on Bhakti Yoga. It contains laconic aphorisms ascribed to Devarishi Narada.

The Holy Rishi Narada propounds the doctrine of love to God, a path which can easily be followed by the ordinary man. It does not demand either great knowledge of philosophy or total renunciation of the world.

Research students will find great help in this book in their study of the Psychology of Bhakti.

The Sutras have an expressible charm and beauty. They make a direct appeal to the heart. Narada speaks to all alike. There is not even the slightest trace or tinge of sectarianism.

And they are the best authority on the Bhakti Marga. For sincere devotees who are in need of practical spiritual instructions, in a very short compass, in the path of devotion or divine love, there is no better book than Narada Bhakti Sutras. The language is very simple.

The Bhakti Sutras of Narada number 84 in all. The first twenty-four of them deal with the nature of Bhakti. The next nine Sutras, i.e., 25 to 33 explain why and how the path of Bhakti is superior to Karma, Jnana and Yoga.

Sutras 34 to 50 (seventeen in all) describe the methods by which Bhakti may be practised and developed.

The next sixteen Sutras (51 to 66) give a description of the external marks by which Bhakti can be detected in a true devotee.

The last 18 Sutras (67 to 84) glorify the great realised souls who are full of devotion to the Lord.

## ORIGIN OF NARADA BHAKTI SUTRAS

Sri Veda Vyasa was staying in his hermitage of Badarikasrama. One day Narada went to the Ashram in the course of his wanderings. Sri Vyasa welcomed the Rishi with due rites and said, "Man seeks freedom, etc. But without devotion it is dry. Devotion is the only way for attaining salvation. All the others have importance only in so far as they are auxiliary to it. I humbly ask you to explain to me the virtue of devotion."

Narada said, "Your disciple Jaimini has already discussed the problem of action in the Purva Mimamsa. You have yourself completed the enquiry of the problem of knowledge in the Uttara Mimamsa. Now you have taken up the problem of devotion. Its full explanation will be given by you in your Srimad Bhagavatam. I shall explain Bhakti in the form of Sutras." So saying Narada delivered a discourse on devotion in 84 aphorisms.

The collection of these Sutras forms a short treatise, known as Narada-Bhakti Sutras (Vide Srimad Bhagavatam (1-4 and 5).

## DEVOTION

The path of Bhakti consists of a gradation of steps. The desire for release from the evil of mortality and the sufferings is its starting point. Para Bhakti or Higher devotion is its goal. It is Para Bhakti that leads to Mukti.

Subsidiary to Para Bhakti, Ekanta-bhava, whole hearted

devotion, there are various forms of devotional states, 81 in number.

Illiterates, females, outcastes—are all equally competent to follow the path of devotion. Desire for release or Mumukshutva is the minimum qualification.

An objector says, God is far above the power of comprehension of man. How, then can one cultivate devotion to Him?

Live in the company of saints. Hear the lilas of God. Study the sacred scriptures. Worship Him first in His several forms as manifested in the world. Worship any image or picture of the Lord or Guru. Recite His name. Sing His glories. You will develop devotion.

According to some, Jnana is instrumental in the cultivation of Bhakti, while others say that they are mutually dependent. But Narada says that Bhakti is the fruit or result of itself.

Devotion is the highest sentiment. Narada has dealt with the subject from the point of view of sentiment alone. Whereas the Bhakti-Mimamsa of Sandilya is an enquiry into the philosophy of devotion. The two treatises are companions. They supplement each other.

When the devotee grows in devotion there is absolute self-forgetfulness. This is called Bhava. Bhava then grows into Maha-Bhava wherein the devotee lives, moves and has his being in the Lord. This is Parama-Prema, the consummation of love or supreme love.

The nine modes of Bhakti have each nine varieties. Therefore Saguna Bhakti becomes eighty-one fold.

By fixing the mind on the Lord through love, hate, fear, friendship, many have attained God-realisation, e.g., the Gopis through love, Kamsa through fear, Sisupala through hate, the Vrishnis through relationship.

Devotion is indicated by Sanmana (honour) as in the case of Arjuna, Bahumana (exaltation) as in the case of Ikshvaku, Prithi (love) as in the case of Vidura, Viraha (pangs of separation) as in the case of Gopis, Itara-vichikitsa (disinclination to others) as in the case of Upamanyu, Mahima-Khyati (glorification) as in the case of Yama, Tadartha-prana-sthana (living for Him) as in the case of Hanuman, Tadiyata (the belief that everything belongs to Him) as in the case of Uparichara Vasu, Sarva-tad-bhava (the consciousness that the Lord is immanent in all things) as in the case of Prahlada, a-pratikula (non-opposition) as in the case of Bhishma.

Bhakti Yoga is the one Yoga which directly appeals to the feelings of man. Apara Bhakti is lower Bhakti. It is a premature stage in devotion. Mature stage of subjective experience is known as Para Bhakti. The devotee has ineffable inner experience of unsurpassing bliss and illumination. He has God-realisation.

There are two stages in Apara or lower Bhakti. The first stage is called Gauna or secondary; the second stage is Mukhya or primary. In Gauna Bhakti there is the influence of Rajo Guna; in Mukhya Bhakti there is influence of Sattva Guna. The mind is calm and serene. Meditation becomes firm and steady. The devotee is in the presence of God. He is conscious of duality.

In Para Bhakti the devotee attains the full grace of the Lord, knowledge and full illumination. He merges in the Lord; he loses his identity. He becomes one with the Lord.

Your happiness depends upon the nature of the object on which you set your heart. The only true object of love is the Lord who is omnipotent, omnipresent and omniscient and all-merciful.

Love of God or devotion is more a practice than a

philosophy. Devotion dethrones the ego and enthrones the Lord in its place. The climax of love is the love of God. Service of the saints, association with the saints, study of Bhakti literature, charity, self-restraint, humility, Japa, Kirtan, prayer—this is the preparation for the love of God.

*Sivananda*

# NAMAPARADHAS

The Glory of the Names of the Lord is indescribable. A devotee should try to avoid the sixty-four offences against Divine Name *(Namaparadhas)*

They are: 1. To recognise God as a deity or a principle, 2. To look upon the Vedas as a book or as having an author, 3. To discriminate between Bhaktas on ground of their caste, 4. To look upon one's preceptor as an ordinary human being, 5. To regard an image or picture of God as wood, stone, metal, paper or clay, 6. To treat Prasada (food offered to the Lord) as ordinary food, 7. To treat Charanamrita (water in which the sacred feet of an image of God have been washed) as ordinary water, 8. To regard Tulsi (the basil plant) as an ordinary plant, 9. To regard the cow as an ordinary beast, 10. To regard the Gita or the Bhagavata as an ordinary book, 11. To regard the Divine sports as human activities , 12. To compare the sports of the Lord with earthly love or sex-pleasure, 13. To regard the Gopis as others' wives (in relation to the Lord), 14. To regard the Rasa dance of Sri Krishna as an amorous sport, 15. To discriminate (between touchables and untouchables) in festivities connected with the Lord, 16. To have no faith in God and the Shastras and to turn an unbeliever, 17. To practise Dharma with a doubting mind, 18. To be slothful in discharging one's religious duties, 19. To judge devotees by external things, 20. To comment on the merits and demerits of saints, 21. To have a high opinion about one's own self, 22. To revile a particular God or scripture, 23. To turn one's back on an image of God. 24. To approach an image of God with shoes on, 25. To wear a garland in the presence of an image of God, 26. To approach an image of God, stick in hand, 27. To approach an image of God, in a blue garment, 28. To approach an image of God, without washing one's mouth and cleaning one's teeth, 29. To enter a temple of God without changing one's clothes, after evacuating one's bowels or sexual intercourse, 30. To stretch one's arms or legs before an image of God. 31. To chew betel-leaves before an image of God, 32. To laugh loudly before an image of God, 33. To make undesirable gesture, 34. To hover around women, 35. To lose one's temper, 36. To salute anyone else in the presence of an image of God, 37. To visit a temple immediately after eating something which gives a foul odour, 38. To insult or assault anyone, 39. To make gestures expressive of lust or anger, 40. To fail in one's duty to a stranger or a holy man, 41. To regard oneself as a devotee, a pious soul, a learned man or a virtuous man, 42. To associate with unbelievers, profligates, sanguinary persons, greedy men and liars, 43. To blame God in adversity, 44. To practise virtue with a sinful motive, 45. To regard oneself as pious even though oppressing anyone even slightly, 46. To refuse to maintain one's wife, children, family, dependents, the needy and holy men, 47. To offer something to God treating it as enjoyable by oneself or to enjoy it without offering it to God beforehand, 48. To swear by the name of one's Ishta Devata, 49. To sell Dharma and the Name of God, 50. To expect anything from anyone else than one's chosen deity, 51. To violate the injunctions of the Sastras, 52. To behave as a knower of Brahman, even though lacking such knowledge, 53. To discriminate between Vaishnavas belonging to different sects, 54. To behave as a God, 55. To revile particular Avataras by discriminating between their respective Lilas, 56. To call anyone as God, even by mistake, 57. To believe God, even by mistake, to be dependent on anyone else, 58. To give the Prasada or Charanamrita of the Lord to anyone through greed, 59. To insult a picture, image or Name of God, 60. To oppress, intimidate or wrong anyone, 61. To renounce faith on losing in a controversy or on one's failure to establish a proposition, 62. To regard the birth and activities of the various Avataras as commonplace, 63. To regard the pair forms of the Deity, such as Sri Radha and Sri Krishna, as distinct or separate, and 64. As an overzealous disciple to act against the spirit of Guru's behest.

# LIFE OF NARADA

## I

Deva Rishi Narada moves about playing on his Veena, singing the praises of Sri Hari drawing the hearts of people towards God thus radiating joy, love and peace throughout the afflicted world. Glory to Devarishi Narada!

Through the power of Yoga he can go wherever he likes in the twinkling of an eye. The misunderstanding and quarrels he creates are all intended for the good of the world. He inspired Valmiki, Vyasa, Sukadeva, Prahlada, Dhruva and other great souls to practise devotion.

Narada was the son of a female servant in his former birth. A large number of saints, sages and Sannyasins came to his village during a certain rainy season to spend their four months of Chaturmas. Narada was a small child at that time. His mother engaged him in their service. He was not childish. He gave up all childish plays. He spoke a very few words. He served them beautifully and wholeheartedly. He served all his time quietly at their feet. The Mahatmas were very much pleased with the boy. They were extremely kind to him. As ordered by them he ate what was left of the food left by them on the leaves. His sins were destroyed by this act. His heart became pure. He heard the beautiful stories of Sri Krishna recited by them. He gradually developed Bhakti. His mind became firm and steady. The Mahatmas gave him special instructions and revealed the secret of divine knowledge.

The Mahatmas left the village. The boy continued to practise Sadhana. He did Bhajan.

One day a snake bit his mother and she died. The boy left the village and went to a dense forest. He sat underneath a Peepul tree on the bank of a river and meditated on Lord Hari.

The Lord revealed Himself in his heart. The hairs of his body stood erect. He forgot all about the world and even the consciousness of his own existence. He was immersed in the ocean of bliss.

Then suddenly the Form of Lord Hari disappeared. The boy was very much grieved. He again tried to have the vision of the Lord. He heard a voice from the sky. "O Child! You cannot again get My vision in the present birth. I revealed Myself to you now in order to increase and strengthen your love towards Me. You have cultivated strong devotion to Me through the influence of Satsanga even for a short time. When you leave your present body, you will be a devotee very near and dear to Me. You will be attached to Me and you will remember through My grace the incidents of your present birth even after the termination of this Kalpa."

The boy left the place and moved about in the world singing the glories and Names of the Lord. He gave up association with the world. In course of time his body perished. He attained the pure, divine body of a companion of God.

At the end of the Kalpa he entered the heart of Brahma through His breath when he lay down on the ocean of dissolution, withdrawing the entire creation within Himself. At the end of a thousand Yugas, he came out from His breath with Maricha and other Rishis, when Brahma began to re-create the world.

Since then, Narada is moving throughout the three worlds playing on the Veena, a gift from God Himself. Whenever Narada merges himself in divine love and sings His sport, that very moment He appears before him.

## II

Narada is endowed with the knowledge of all the truths of the Vedas. He knows Dharma well. He has perfect knowledge of Itihasas and Puranas. He has knowledge of the facts of the previous Kalpa. He is a master of music. He is an eloquent speaker. He possesses a direct vision of all the regions through his power of Yoga. He creates quarrels for the good of the world. He is a great teacher of Devotion. He is the very embodiment of devotion.

Narada is one of the wisest among the sages. He is ever engaged in austerities. He is a divine ministrel. He is a great ascetic. He rose from a low position to the highest spiritual glory through divine grace and self effort. He is a Jnani, Yogi and Bhakta in one.

He is a knower of Brahman. He is a seer of Vedic Mantras. He is a saviour. He is a reformer. He is honoured everywhere. He is a great master in the art of reconciling others. He is endowed with intellectual penetration, tact, humility, forbearance, tranquillity, self-control, truthfulness, compassion, firm love for God. He is ever doing what is auspicious.

He is one of the ten spiritual sons of Brahma. He went to Sanatkumara for attaining wisdom. He admitted that his vast erudition could not remove the burden of sorrow. Therefore Sanatkumara illumined him about the Infinite Bliss; Bhuma, vide Chhandogya Upanishad.

Narada is the friend, philosopher, guide and consoler of all—Gods, demons and men.

Through the grace of Narada, Dhruva was enthroned permanently in his celestial state. Narada takes into his care Hiranya's wife who was then carrying Prahlada.

He advises the demon Andhaka to test the power of Siva's boon on himself. He advises Kamsa to slay the children of Devaki. He manages to get Ravana entangled on Vali's tail. He goes as a messenger to Indra from Sri Krishna to remove his pride by depriving him of the Parijata. These incidents reveal the greatness of his character.

Various scriptures name Devarishi Narada as the third Avatara of Lord Hari. In the third chapter of Srimad Bhagavatam which gives the list of 22 incarnations, he comes after Purusha and Varaha.

Narada has been a source of noble and valuable inspiration to those who have sought him and found him.

May the blessings of Devarishi Narada be upon you all!

### NARADA INSPIRES SRI VYASA

Maharishi Vyasa divided the Vedas into four parts for the benefit of the people at large. He composed the Mahabharata. He wrote the 18 Puranas and yet he was not quite satisfied. He had no peace of mind. He went to the bank of the river Saraswati and sat there in a reflective mood.

Narada appeared before him and said "O Maharishi! In your books you have not sung the praise of God to the extent you described the other aspects of Dharma. You have failed to deal at length the Bhagavata Dharma. That is the reason why you are restless now. Now describe the Lilas of Sri Krishna for the good of the world. You will enjoy everlasting peace." Sri Vyasa at once began to write Bhagavatam."

### DAKSHA'S CURSE ON NARADA

At the beginning of creation, Daksha procreated 10,000 children through his wife Asikni, daughter of Pancajanya, in order to populate the whole world. These children of Daksha called Haryasvas went on a pilgrimage to Narayanasaras. They wanted to carry out the orders of their father. Narada advised them to attain self-realisation, the highest goal of life. They became sannyasins and never returned to the worldly life.

Daksha became very angry. Brahma consoled him. He again procreated 10,000 children called Sabalasvas. They too went to Narayanasaras. They too became absorbed in God and never returned.

Daksha cursed Narada. Narada is ever a wanderer without a permanent abode owing to the force of Daksha's curse. He wanders all over the world.

# CONTENTS

# NARADA BHAKTI
# SUTRAS

**Om Sat Guru Paramatmane Namah.**
**Om Sri Ganesaya Namah.**
**Om Sarasvatyai Namah.**
**Salutations to Deva Rishi Narada.**

## THE NATURE OF DIVINE LOVE

अथातो भक्ति व्याख्यास्यामः ॥१॥

**Sutra 1. Athato bhaktim vyakhyasyamah.**

*Now, therefore, we shall expound Bhakti (devotion).*

अथ Atha: now, अतः Atah: therefore, भक्तिम् Bhaktim:
(the doctrine of) devotion, व्याख्यास्यामः Vyakhyasyamah:
(we) shall expound.

Sutra means an aphorism or terse saying impregnant
with deep significance. Just as flowers or pearls are arranged or studded on a thread, so also philosophical ideas
are studded or spread or arranged in the aphorism. Rishis
always have expressed their ideas in the form of laconic
Sutras. That is the beauty in the writings of Rishis or seers.
That is the sign of God-realisation. The six *Dharsanas* or
schools of philosophy are embodied in the form of Sutras
only. Without a commentary it is difficult for laymen to understand these Sutras.

'Atha' means now. It is sometimes used in the sense
of sequence. It is a word that is used when a subject is
begun to invoke the Divine blessing and for the proper
closing of the work undertaken. It also implies completion
of the preliminary conditions. An aspirant cannot take to

the deep study of philosophy and spiritual practice without preparation, without proper qualifications.

The aspirant must be endowed with aspiration, faith, devotion, tolerance, patience, perseverance, forgiveness, mercy, serenity, cheerfulness, courage, non-violence, truthfulness, purity or Brahmacharya, spirit of self-less service, dispassion, renunciation and one-pointed mind. This is the preparation for the love of God.

The aspirant should have faith in the grace of God. He must have intense desire to attain God-realisation. He must have deep faith in the scripture and in the capacity of the Teacher. He must have the capacity to understand. He must be free from disabilities and must have all possible opportunities and favourable circumstances. Then alone he is fit to practise Bhakti. Then alone he will be profited.

Ramanuja, the founder of the Visishtadvaita school of philosophy mentions seven qualifications as being indispensable for those who wish to follow the path of devotion. They are: — 1. *Viveka* (discrimination in food), 2. *Vimoka* (freedom from desires), 3. *Abhyasa* (practice), 4. *Kriya* or the habit of doing good to others, 5. *Kalyana*, purity in thought, word and deed, non-violence, charity and other virtues. 6. *Anavasada* (cheerfulness) and 7. *Anuddharsa* or absence of excessive hilarity

**Atha,** Now: indicates that Narada Rishi is now entering into the exposition of the nature of Bhakti and the means of attaining it, after having already expounded the other cults and disciplines of Karma, Janana, etc.

**Atah,** Therefore, alludes to the reason that prompted Narada to propound the Bhakti Sastra, viz. Bhakti itself leads to God-realisation and escape from samsara. It is the easiest path. It can be followed by any one. It is a help to those who aspire for Jnana. Even Jnanis like Sankara, Madhu Sudhana, Suka Dev took to Bhakti after realisation to enjoy the sweetness and loving relationship with God. Narada himself likes Bhakti most and is eager to share his bliss of love with others.

The term Bhakti comes from the root 'Bhaj', which means "to be attached to God." Bhajan, worship, Bhakti, Anurag, Prem, Prithi are synonymous terms. Bhakti is love for love's sake. The devotee wants God and God alone. There is no selfish expectation here.

**Vyakhyasyamah:** This means literally 'shall comment upon'. This work is not a commentary in the usual sense of the term. It is a commentary on the actual experiences of the devotees. It is not a mere speculative philosophical exposition, based on other's experiences. It is the exposition based on the author's own personal experiences, supported by scriptures.

# DEFINITION OF BHAKTI

सा त्वस्मिन् परमप्रेमरूपा ॥२॥

**Sutra 2. Sa tvasmin parama-prema-rupa.**

*That (devotion), verily, is of the nature of supreme Love of God.*

सा Sa: That (i.e., Bhakti); तु tu: But; अस्मिन् Asmin: in this; परम Parama: Supreme; प्रेम Prema: Love; रूपा Rupa: Form.

Some read Tasmin or Kasmai in place of tvasmin.

Sandilya's definition of Bhakti is सा परानुरक्तिरीश्वरे "absolute attachment to God."

The term Bhakti comes from the root "Bhaj", which means "to be attached to God." Bhajan, worship, Bhakti, Anurag, Prem, Prithi are synonymous terms. Bhakti is love for love's sake. The devotee wants God and God alone. There is no selfish expectation here. There is no fear also. Therefore, it is called *"Parama Prem Rupa."* Is the son afraid of his father, who is a Sessions Judge? Is the wife afraid of her husband? So also a devotee entertains the least fear of God. The fear of retribution vanished in him. He feels, believes, conceives and imagines that his Ishtam is an Ocean of Love or Prem.

Devotion or Bhakti is exclusive love for God. The devotee wants God and God alone. He is completely attached to God. He has no attraction or love for any object in this world. He is absolutely free from all mundane desires. He has no desire for the enjoyment of the next world. He does not want even Mukti.

Supreme Love does not seek a return. It does not expect a reward. The lover wants his Beloved alone. The devotee is quite indifferent to the pleasures of this world. He has no interest in the affairs of this world.

Mark how love develops. First arises faith. Then follows attraction and after that adoration. Adoration leads to suppression of mundane desires. The result is single-mindedness and satisfaction. Then grow attachment and supreme love towards God.

In this type of highest Bhakti all attraction and attachment which one has for objects of enjoyment are transferred to the only dearest object, viz., God. This leads the devotee to an eternal union with his Beloved and culminates in oneness.

Bhakti is divided into two kinds, viz., Apara Bhakti or Gauna Bhakti and Para Bhakti. Apara Bhakti is the lower or initial stage of devotion of an aspirant following the path of Bhakti, while Para Bhakti is the highest stage of Bhakti.

The relationship of the devotee with the Lord in various stages is beautifully described here. Sri Hanuman says to Lord Rama, देहबुध्या तु दासोऽहं जीवबुध्या त्वदंशकः । आत्मबुध्या त्वमेवाहमिति मे निश्चिता मतिः "when I think of myself as an embodied being, I am your servant; when I think of myself as an individual soul, I am part of you; but when I realise 'I am Atman' I am one with you. This is my firm conviction."

Love grows wildly in the ignorant man's heart. There is a luscious fruit of love in a corner of the heart, but the entire heart is strewn with thorns of hatred, jealousy and so many other vicious qualities that the charm of love is marred. There are the bushes of lust, anger and greed, which hide within them the wildest animals. Love lies hidden far beneath and far beyond reach. It is as good as non-existent. But, in the case of a true devotee of the Lord, this love has been cultured, and the garden of his heart is cleared of the thorns of vicious qualities, of the bushes of lust, anger and greed. Love of God which is the sweetest of fragrances wafts from such a heart.

तु (Tu) is used to differentiate the highest Bhakti which Maharshi Narada alludes to in this Sutra from the lower type of devotion which is actuated by ulterior motives and desires or fear of God, etc.

You should know the difference between ordinary love, the love between wife and husband, children and parents, friends and relations.

The word अस्मिन् (asmin) is used in this Sutra to denote the object of love. Narada's teaching is non-sectarian. He did not use the word, Brahman, Iswar, Rama, Krishan, Siva, etc.

**Parama-Prema-Rupa:** There is no trace of selfishness or egoism or any motive or fear in this kind of supreme love. Do not mistake emotion or fanaticism for devotion or supreme love. It will pass away soon. Blind faith also is not supreme love.

The various objects which devotees worship according to their spiritual development are: 1. A Personal God, Vishnu, Siva, etc., 2. An idol or image of the Personal God which will remind him of the Personal God, 3. An Avatara like Lord Rama or Lord Krishna, 4. Guru or one's spiritual guide, 5. Humanity in general, 6. The whole world (Visvarupa) conceived as the manifestation of the Supreme

Being, 7. The Antaryamin or the inner ruler or controller of all the objects in the world, 8. One's own Atman.

अमृतस्वरूपा च ॥३ ॥

**Sutra 3. Amritasvarupa cha.**

*And it is of the nature of nectar.*

अमृत स्वरूपा Amritasvarupa: Of the nature of nectar; च cha: and,

Devotion is real nectar. It secures freedom from the wheel of births and deaths. Lord Yama cannot come near a devotee. The devotee attains immortality. He lives constantly in the presence of God.

Amrita: "A" means "not" and "Mrita" means death. Amrita is that which bestows immortality.

God, Immortality (*Amritam*), Peace (*Santi*), Absolute, Infinite (*ananta*), intelligence, Consciousness (*chit*), Eternity, Bliss (*ananda*), Nirvana, Freedom (*Mukti*) Perfection (*Siddhi*) are synonymous terms.

Devotion gives Immortality. Bhakti is an embodiment of Amrita or nectar. *Nitya Sukha* (eternal bliss), Immortality, *Param Santi* (supreme peace). *Nitya Tripti* (eternal satisfaction), *Akhanda Sukha* (unbroken joy) can be had only in God. That is the reason why aspirants attempt for God realisation. Worldly pleasure is not constant. He who smiles and laughs for five minutes weeps bitterly for hours together. No man in this world is perfectly happy. A multi-millionaire is full of cares, worries, anxieties and fear. He is afraid of enemies. He is guarded by sepoys. He has to take injection for getting sleep, as he is always worried. He is worse than a prisoner. Rockefeller, the richest man in the world, who could pave a road of several miles with golden sheets, expressed to a priest who went to behold his glory and opulence: " O revered priest ! I am the most miserable man in the world. I cannot eat anything; my stomach, kidneys and liver are filled with germs and diseases. I am always restless." Maitreyi puts a question to her husband, Yajnavalkya, "O My Lord ! can the wealth of the three worlds give me immortality?" Yajnavalkya replied, Certainly not, my beloved." Yama also says to Nachiketas: "Wealthy people on account of delusion and pride lose their memory, intellect and understanding, and go round and round in this impermanent and unhappy world and come again and again into my clutches. Wealth and woman are the two snares to entrap the worldly-minded persons whose minds are filled with lust and greed. You are above these things. You have shunned all my temptations. You have selected the " Sreya Marga."

This is the world of diversity. Intellects are different. Faces are different. Religions are different. Sounds are different. Faiths are different. Tastes and temperaments are different. But one thing is common in all. Every one of us wants *Nitya Sukha* (eternal happiness), infinite knowledge, immortality, freedom and independence. These things can be obtained by God-realisation alone.

# FRUITS OF BHAKTI

## यल्लब्ध्वा पुमान् सिद्धो भवति अमृतो भवति
## तृप्तो भवति ॥४॥

**Sutra 4. Yallabdhva puman siddho bhavati, amrito bhavati, tripto bhavati.**

*On attaining it (this supreme love) man becomes perfect, immortal and (fully) satisfied.*

यत् Yat: which; लब्ध्वा Labdhava: having attained; पुमान् Puman: man; सिद्ध Siddah: perfect; भवति becomes; अमृत Amrita. Immortal; भवति Bhavati: becomes; तृप्त Triptah: satisfied; भवति Bhavati: becomes.

Sutras 4, 5 and 6 describe the fruits of Bhakti.

**Puman:** The word Puman is specially significant. It means any man. The practice of Bhakti and the attainment of Mukti are not restricted by any considerations of caste, creed, colour, sex, or country. Every human being who has faith, devotion and aspiration can cultivate Bhakti and attain God-realisation through Bhakti. Even Nandan, Dharma Vyadha, Raidas, Kabir attained God-realisation. Puranas speak of even animals getting the grace of the Lord. There is the account of Gajendra.

**Siddho Bhavati:** The devotee becomes perfect through God-realisation. His object is attained. All his desires are gratified by God-realisation. He never feels the want of anything. He enjoys supreme peace, eternal and perfect satisfaction and ever-lasting bliss and so he becomes a Siddha.

For a devotee, Siddhis or powers are worthless. He does not care for them. These are nothing when compared to Divine Love. He rejects even the position of Indra or Brahma, even Mukti or liberation. His mind is filled with divine ecstasy. He has realised the whole.

He has realised the essence and totality of all. He has attained the source and fountain of all. And so he is perfect, immortal and thoroughly satisfied. He cannot be attracted towards external objects, which are incomplete, imperfect, defective and are only parts.

A Siddha is a perfect man. He has reached the goal. He has attained God-realisation. In common parlance the word Siddha denotes a man who is endowed with various superhuman powers or Siddhis. It is not in any such sense the word is used here. The sign of a perfect man or Siddha is not the possession of miraculous powers but the attainment of God-realisation or unity with the Supreme Being.

**Amrito Bhavati:** He who has attained God-realisation becomes immortal. He ever lives in the presence of God. He has his being in God. He has no more desires and so he will not take any more body or birth. Immortality, *Amritatva*, constitutes the essential nature of Bhakti.

**Tripto Bhavati:** A devotee who is a Siddha or who is perfect and who is immortal is absolutely satisfied.

Contentment here referred to is not the kind of satisfaction which one gets when some desire is fulfilled. It is absolute satisfaction that comes from the absence of all desires and the attainment of God-realisation. Only when one attains the highest perfection can one be perfectly satisfied in his own Self. Only then can one be contented with oneself. There is no other gain superior to that absolute satisfaction attained through God-realisation.

He who has the philosopher's stone cares not for little

pieces of gold. Even so a devotee who has reached the fountain-source of everything cares not for the little objects of this world.

The devotee loves God and serves Him and His creation. He does not strive consciously for Mukti but God confers Mukti on His devotee unsolicited.

All weakness and Doshas (faults) vanish. People put a question: "How can we love God whom we have not seen?" Remain in the company of Bhaktas; hear the Lila of Bhagavan, His *Aiswarya* (Divine Powers) or *Vibhutis*, His *Madhurya* (grace and beauty); serve Bhaktas; sing His names daily and do Japa of His Mantra; stay for one year in Ayodhya or Brindavan or Chitrakute or Pandharpur, Banaras or Ananda Kutir. You will develop love for God.

यत्राप्य न किञ्चिद्वाञ्छति न शोचति न द्वेष्टि न रमते
नोत्साही भवति ॥५॥

**Sutra 5. Yatprapya na Kinchidvanchati na sochati na dveshti na ramate notsahi bhavati.**

*By attaining which (divine love) he does not desire anything else, neither grieves (over any loss or death of dear ones) nor hates anything, does not indulge in sensual pleasures, nor does he feel any urge (for the acquisition of material things).*

यत् Yat: which (love of God); प्राप्य Praapya: having obtained; पुमान् puman: (a person); न na: not; किञ्चित् kinchit: anything; वाञ्छति vanchati: desires; न na: not; शोचति Sochati: grieves: न Na: not; द्वेष्टि Dveshti: feels enmity; न na: not; रमते Ramate: rejoices; उत्साही Utsahi: one who is active (in one's own interest); न भवति Na Bhavati: does not become or is not.

**Labhdva:** in the previous Sutra (having gained) and **Prapya** (having attained) in the present one are apparently similar in meaning, yet, there is a subtle distinction. Attainment involves personal effort. Labha or gain on the contrary may come unexpectedly.

Now Rishi Narada describes the negative aspect of divine love.

**Na Kinchit Vanchati:** A devotee rises above all earthly wants. His heart is full of supreme Peace and perfect satisfaction. Therefore, he does not desire anything else. He is conscious of the unreality and illusory nature of worldly objects. Hence he does not take any interest in them. His thirst for sensual pleasure has been quenched for ever by the attainment of God-realisation. His heart is full now. Kingdom, wealth, power, etc., have no attraction for him.

Why does desire manifest? On account of Avidya or ignorance or imperfection or lack of bliss. When one gets Darshan of God, all desires are burnt up. When the boy Dhruva had Darshan of Lord Hari, the desire to obtain kingdom that prompted him to worship the Lord disappeared. Devotion is a fire like Gyanagni (fire of wisdom) that burns up all mundane desires.

Desires arise from a sense of imperfection or limitation. The feeling of imperfection is possible only when a man finds something outside himself, other than himself. When the devotee attains God-realisation he is not conscious of anything other than God. Therefore, a devotee becomes absolutely desireless.

**Na Sochati:** A devotee has no grief. He has no particular attachment to any object or person. He expects nothing, hopes nothing, fears nothing. He has no disappointment, frustration or failure or loss. Therefore, he has no grief.

The devotee who realises God is freed from grief also. Can darkness remain in the presence of light? How can sorrow manifest when one is immersed in the Ocean of Bliss and Prem? Grief is a mental creation. It manifests when the mind is attached to the body and illusory connections. When the mind is obliterated, when there is self-absorption and self-effacement by merging in the bosom of God, how can grief approach the devotee? Absolutely impossible.

**Na Dveshti:** Freedom from hatred is the next sign of perfect man or realised devotee. When the devotee is free from desire and pain, when he beholds God in all forms, he cannot have hatred for any creature. He feels that if he hates anybody, he hates God Himself.

A devotee hates none. He loves all, serves all and helps all. He is ever engaged in the good of all beings. He works for the enlightenment and uplift of the lesser, unfortunate infant souls.

He is not attached to any person, object or place. He tastes the honey of divine love and so he does not depend on any worldly object for his personal satisfaction.

The devotee does not hate anything. Hatred is due to ignorance. How can the devotee hate anybody when he sees Lord Hari in everything? He feels that the world is a manifestation of the Lord and all movements and actions are His Lila. He has no *Ghrina* or dislike for fecal matter, dirt, *Chandala*, scavenger, cobbler, beggar, prostitute, thief, etc. He says, "I see everywhere my sweet Lord. It is Hari who is playing the part of prostitute, thief, dacoit, scavenger." He has an all-embracing, all inclusive, exalted mental state. This cannot be adequately described in words. It has to be felt. Mira, Gouranga, Hafiz, Tulasidas, Kabir, Ramadas all enjoyed this state. Tulasidas says, *"Sitaramamaya sab jaga jani karou pranam jori juga pani" — Knowing the whole world to be the manifestation of Sita and Rama, I prostrate to all with hands bowed in worship."*

In Purusha Sukta you will find a description of the Purusha: "The Purusha has one thousand heads, one thousand eyes, one thousand feet." There is an echo of these ideas in the Gita, Ch. XIII – 13. "Everywhere that hath hands and feet, everywhere eyes, heads and mouths: all-hearing. He dwelt in the world enveloping all." Lord Krishna gives advice to Uddhava and prescribes an easy way for reaching Him. "Know, Uddhava, that Brahmin, Chandala, ass, dog, king, beggar are all my forms. When you meet any object, do prostration and feel My presence." Nam Dev said to the dog; "O Vittala, my dear, in the form of dog, do not run away with the dry bread. It will affect your soft throat. Pray, let me apply ghee to the bread." He ran with ghee in a cup to the dog. Sri Ramakrishna Paramahamsa prostrated before an out-caste girl: "O Mother Kali! I see Thee in this girl". Pravahari Baba prostrated before a thief with a bag of utensils: "O thief Narayana! Pray, accept these things. I never knew that thief Narayana was in my cottage." Ekanath, a Maharashtra Bhakta, gave his ring voluntarily to the thief when he entered the house. "O thief! take this ring also. Your Kartavya (duty) is to steal the things. Thou art Krishna. Keep up this Lila." Have you understood the sublime state of these exalted Bhaktas who have a new angle of vision? A day will come to you also. Exert. Struggle.

**Na Utsahi Bhavati:** A devotee does not work to promote his own self-interest but works for the good of all without any sense of ego or of any feeling of external compulsion, in a spirit of service to God. As he is not prompted by ego, as he does not wish for fruits, his actions are no actions at all.

He does not work for his personal pleasure and profit. He has no enthusiasm for selfish or worldly pursuits. He is not affected by success and failure.

How can a devotee be enthusiastic about anything? A man undertakes a work on account of pleasure in it or of the pleasure that it will bring. There is no more work to be done by a devotee of God-realisation. He enjoys the highest bliss.

When the devotee has the fountain of all bliss by his side, how can there be any desire in him for the enjoyment of worthless and trivial sensual pleasure?

How can a trace of earthly desire remain when God, the embodiment of bliss is attained by the devotee? Darshan of God comes in various ways, viz. in dreams, in physical form as ordinary man, in physical form with four hands with conch, mace, discus and lotus-flower in the hands, in the form of cosmic consciousness which Arjuna had, in the form of Hiranyagarbha consciousness or full Knowledge of Brhama Loka, etc. Note how Arjuna expresses his experiences of cosmic consciousness. "Nor source, nor midst, nor end; infinite force, unnumbered arms, the Sun and Moon Thine eyes; I see Thy face, as sacrificial fire, blazing its splendor burneth up the worlds." God sometimes gives Darshan to encourage His devotee by coming down in *Viman* (celestial car). *Akasa Vani*, dazzling lights in space or sky are some other encouragements which God gives to push His devotees on the path vigorously and rapidly. The devotee should not stop his Sadhana on account of false *Tushti* (satisfaction) when he gets His Darshan. He should ever rest in God. He should have perfect

*Nishta* in God always (Svaroop-sthiti). He should not leave off his practices till he merges himself in the Lord in *Maha-Bhava* or *Tanmaya* state.

Give up this unquenchable thirst for sensual pleasure, woman, money and worldly prosperity, which is the greatest obstacle in the path of devotion, and turn your mind towards God. Here is an inexhaustible and imperishable spiritual wealth which no decoit can rob; a Divine Bliss which is not mixed with fear or pain.

## II

Now everything becomes natural, effortless and automatic. Effort is necessary only as long as the ego or the feeling of separateness persists. When these are removed and when the Light of the Divine has descended into the devotee, he puts forth no more effort. This is confirmed by the Lord in the Bhagavad Gita (vide chapter II – 59). "The objects of the sense turn away from the abstinent man leaving the longing behind but his longing also turns away on seeing the Supreme."

He does not desire or crave for anything because he has no ego, he is filled with Divine Love and he therefore feels no want. Desire exists only so long as the ego or the sense of separateness with its concomitant imperfection exists. When this state is transcended, in Para Bhakti, all desires come to an end, they find their fulfilment in the Lord. Compared to the invaluable treasure of divine love, the wealth of the three worlds appears to be a straw in the eyes of the Bhakta; what to speak of motor cars, bungalows, name, fame or other worldly possessions. The sum-total of all the pleasures of the universe is like a drop when compared to the ocean of Bliss; i.e., God, who is the source of all these pleasures. Nothing tempts the Bhakta who has attained His Love. As a man who gets nectar to drink will not be tempted to drink in a muddy pool of water, just as a man who gets a bagful of sugar-candy will not hanker after black-jaggery, so also a devotee who has got that Supreme Bhakti will not hanker after anything whatsoever.

Grief results from attachment and desire. When the devotee does not desire anything, not even Liberation, will he grieve for the loss of any possession? On the other hand, he will willingly renounce everything, for the sake of attaining God and His Love.

When there is neither craving nor grief, there can exist neither elation nor hatred—for these two pairs follow each other. Hatred and sense-delight are rooted in desire, its frustration or its fulfilment respectively. When the Bhakta is always immersed in the thought of his Beloved (God) and sees Him alone in everything and in every being, how can he hate anybody? And, when there is nothing greater than God, how can anything other than God cause elation in him?

When the devotee has attained Eternal Satisfaction in His Love, the impulse for attaining something else disappears and with it the desire to perform actions for the achievement of any personal gains. Only as long as there is a sense of imperfection can there be a motive for action. In Divine Love the Bhakta achieves Perfection. He sees the Lord in all, and all in God. Therefore he ceases to perform actions of his own volition. A similar idea is expressed in the Bhagavad Gita, "He who neither rejoices nor hates, nor grieves, nor desires, renouncing good and evil, full of devotion, he is dear to Me." (Chapter XII—17).

Thenceforward, he becomes the instrument of God; he performs actions without his own Sankalpa, without desire or attachment, in accordance with His Will for the well-being of the whole world.

Therefore, attain that Love of God in this very instant. All your sorrows, desires, cravings, fear and anxieties will come to an end. You will become perfect and you will enjoy eternal satisfaction. You will be immersed in Perennial Bliss.

यज्ज्ञात्वा मत्तो भवति स्तब्धो भवत्यात्मारामो भवति ॥६॥

**Sutra 6. Yajjnatva matto bhavati sthabdho bhavatyatmaramo bhavati.**

*By knowing which man becomes intoxicated (or overjoyed), peaceful and completely immersed in the enjoyment of the Bliss of the Atman.*

यत् Yat: which (God); ज्ञात्वा Jnatva: having known; पुमान् Puman: (A person) मत्तः Mattah: Intoxicated; overjoyed; भवति Bhavati: Becomes; (Iva: as it were) स्तब्धः Sthabdha: quiet, भवति becomes; आत्मारामः Aatmaramah: one continually enjoying the bliss of the Atman; भवति Bhavati: becomes.

The description of a realised devotee is continued.

In this Sutra the author says, "By knowing That" – by "That" he means God. But in the previous Sutra he says, "On obtaining That" – and there he means love.

**Jnatva:** Previous expressions were "Labdhva" 'having gained' and 'Prapya' 'having attained'. Now it is "having known."

**Matto Bhavati:** The devotee gets thoroughly intoxicated with the divine love. He spends his days and nights in singing the praises of the Lord and in hearing His glory.

He remains merged in the Lord, also he is not conscious of the external world.

He now laughs, now weeps, now cries, now sings aloud and now begins to dance in divine ecstasy. Through excess of joy he gets horripilation. Sometimes he becomes silent and sits motionless like a statue.

This is the state of identity or union with the Lord. The devotee loses his separate existence. He has no will of his own as he has already surrendered it completely to the Lord. He is simply an instrument in the hands of the Lord.

One of the Nayanars burnt up his hair on the head when he was not able to get oil for burning the light in the temple.

Another cut off the nose of a queen who had plucked up a flower and smelt it when the devotee was making a garland of flowers to be offered to Siva. The queen's husband came and cut off her hand which he said had committed the first offence, because it had picked up the flowers.

A Nayanar or devotee rubbed his elbow on the sandal stone when he could not get any more sandal wood for the use of Lord Siva.

St. Francis of Assisi brought upon himself, through intense meditation on Lord Jesus Christ, the marks of crucifixion and joyfully experienced the extreme pain to which Jesus himself had been subjected at the time of crucifixion.

In the Upanishads Atman is compared to Madhu or honey. The Sufis often compare it to wine; the Saktas compare it to liquor. In the Vedic Yajna it is Soma Juice. All these symbolise the enjoyment of the sweetness of divine bliss.

A devotee who was drunk the wine of divine love cannot observe the conventional rules of propriety. He is not a slave to the conventional laws of society and scriptures. The God-intoxicated devotee is not conscious of himself.

**Stabdha bhavati:** When a devotee acts, it is God who acts through him. A devotee is inwardly quite peaceful and serene when serves the world out of love and mercy.

**Atmaramo bhavati:** The devotee grows into the likeness of the Lord and therefore shares with Him His perfection and partakes of His infinite bliss and joy. He realised the Atman within and beholds the Atman in every creature.

When one is happy in his own Self, then alone he becomes independent. If one depends for his happiness on perishable objects, he begins to weep when the centre of his pleasure is withdrawn. The husband weeps when his wife or son dies, when the bank in which he has deposited his money fails. Objects that are conditioned in time, space and causation are Vinasi, perishable. They cannot give, therefore, eternal happiness to human beings. So in the Gita Bhagavan Sri Krishna says: "The delights that are contact-born, they are verily wombs of pain, for they have beginning and ending, O Kaunteya, not in them the wise may rejoice. Ch. V-22. That which from the union of the senses with their objects at first is as nectar, but in the end is like venom, is Rajasic Sukha, not real happiness. But he whose Self is unattached to external contacts and findeth joy in the Self, having the self harmonised with the Eternal by Yoga, enjoys happiness exempt from decay (Ch. XVIII-38 and V. 21). "The man who rejoiceth in the Self, with the

Self is satisfied, and is content in the Self, for him verily there is nothing to do." Ch. III-17. Nothing can shake a man who rejoices in the Self (Atmarati); who is satisfied in the Self (Atma tripta); and who is contented in the Self (Atma Santushti); and who plays in the Self (Atma Kreeda).

It is Vasana (subtle desire) that draws a man outside towards external objects. Avidya (ignorance) has got two forces, the Avarana or veiling power, the Sakti that screens the man from his real Satchitananda Svarupa behind and the Vikshepa Sakti that makes the mind and senses outgoing. The restlessness of the mind is due to desire and Vikshepa Sakti. Avidya clouds the understanding and produces intoxication, destroys the intellect and makes the intellect perverted, stony and barren. Therefore, man always thinks that he can get pleasure in external objects, mistakes the body, children and wife as Atma and takes the unreal world as real. When lust manifests, the intellect becomes blind and the most intelligent man becomes an easy prey to passion. A worldly-minded man vainly searches for his happiness in outside perishable objects. The idea that he should dive deep into the chambers of his heart — by collecting all the dispersed rays of the mind, and withdrawing the out-going senses — and meditate on God, never strikes him. He never believes in devotion, concentration and meditation. He cannot imagine of a pure, unalloyed happiness that is independent of external objects, although he enjoys the bliss of the Self daily at night. He foolishly thinks: "If I have a son, if I have a garden, I will be happy." The tendency of the mind is such that it tries to seek happiness outside in perishable objects. This is due to the force of Avidya.

But the devotee gets the grace of the Lord. His intellect is calm and tranquil. All the outgoing energies become transmuted into spiritual energy. He gets help and strength from Mantra Sakti, Sadhana Sakti and Upasana Shakti. Sattva flows from the feet of the Lord towards his mind. All desires melt away. The Vikshepa Sakti is destroyed. He has the firm, unshakable conviction that the real happiness is in God. His mind is always inward. He has *Antarmukh vritti.* The senses do not wander about. They get absorbed in the mind and the mind gets absorbed in God. He is ever peaceful. He enjoys the happiness within. He delights in the bliss of God. He, therefore, stands adamant even amidst grave troubles and calamities. So Rishi Narada uses the expressions "Stabdho Bhavati." The devotee becomes serene and "Atmaaramo bhavati" (happy in the bliss of the Self).

The devotee gets divine intoxication. Lord Gouranga was so much intoxicated with the divine nectar of *Prem* that sometimes he did not know when it was day-break and when it was night. Mira, though a young Rani, danced in the streets amidst males and men of inferior class on account of this intoxication of Krishna Prem.

Sri Ramakrishna Paramahamsa remained in the thick jungle for four days without taking any food when he was under this divine intocxication. Words can hardly describe the nature of this divine intoxication. One has to feel it oneself. Even if there is a mild intoxication it will give immense strength to the devotee to face the difficulties in the battle of life. Therefore Narada says, "Matto Bhavati."

# RENUNCIATION

## सा न कामयमाना निरोधरूपत्वात् ॥७॥

**Sutra 7. Sa na kamayamana nirodharupatvat.**

*Bhakti (supreme love) is not of the nature of lust (desire), because it is of the form of renunciation.*

सा Sa: it; that (i.e., Bhakti described as Paramapremarupa in Sutra 2); न na: not; कामयमाना Kamayamana: of the nature of lust; निरोधरूपत्वात् Nirodharupatvat: being of the form of renunciation.

Bhakti is no worldly desires. The moment Bhakti dawns all desires disappear. The devotee does not expect any reward from God. He loves Him for love's sake.

Devotion to the Lord is not certainly for one's own gain. The basis of Bhakti is self-restraint. Renunciation is the very essence of this devotional love. Divine love has no element of desire in it.

Bhakti is not led by desires, for it finds expression in the inhibition of all desires. The inhibition of all desires is not a total annihilation or extinction of all activities.

Devotion cannot co-exist with desire of any kind, not even the desire for liberation. The devotee wants God and God alone and His Service. He does not accept even when offered the five forms of Mukti.

**Kamayamana:** It means "of the nature of Kama." "Kama" is not only sexual lust but desire in general. Bhakti Yoga is not practiced for any selfish purpose whatsoever.

The devotee does not want prosperity, power or even release from pain and sufferings. The basis of devotion or divine love is self-denial.

Desire obstructs the growth of devotion. Devotion to the Lord increases in intensity when mundane desires are renounced.

The psychologists and psychiatrists foolishly imagine that spiritual experience is of sexual origin. It is a terrible mistake. It is purely divine.

It is not a suppressed experience of sexuality.

Continence of a spiritual aspirant is not repression or suppression. It is sublimation of sex-energy into *ojas* or spiritual energy which is utilised in divine contemplation.

Prahlada, Dhruva, Nachiketas showed signs of spiritual illumination even from boyhood.

Desire is an enemy of peace. Desire is an enemy of devotion. Without renunciation (*tyaga*) Bhakti can never be cultivated in the heart. *Vishaya Asakti* (attachment to sensual enjoyments) is the greatest obstacle in developing devotion. Energy leaks out. No improvement is seen in spiritual Sadhana. The devotee always complains: "I have not realised anything in the path of devotion. My mind remains in the same state. It always wanders about wildly in sensual grooves. I am restless. What is to be done?" Desire is very powerful. It assumes various subtle forms. Desire is Maya's weapon to hurl down the Jivas in the mire of Samsara. There is no end for desires. It is unconquerable. Enjoyment does not bring satisfaction of a desire. Just as fire is increased by pouring ghee over it so also desire is strengthened by *Bhoga*. Have you not studied the life of Raja Yayati in Mahabharata? He borrowed the youthful state from his son and enjoyed for thousands of years and cried out in the end: "Alas! My passion has not gone. There is no satiety. My heart is still burning with lust." Bhartrihari weeps bitterly: " I have renounced the world, wife and kingdom. I live on leaves and water. I do penance, yet lust is troubling me." Such is the potency of desire.

That is the reason why Lord Krishna says in the Gita: "Enveloped is wisdom by this constant enemy of the wise in the form of desire, which is insatiable as a flame. The senses, the mind and the reason are said to be its seat; by these, enveloping wisdom, it bewilders the dweller in the body. Therefore, O best of the Bharatas, mastering first the senses do thou slay this thing of sin, destructive of wisdom and knowledge. Thus understanding Him greater than the Reason restraining the self by the self, slay thou, O mighty-armed, the enemy in the form of desire, difficult to overcome. When a man abandoneth, O Partha, all the desires of the heart, and is satisfied in the self, by the Self, then is he called stable in mind." Chapt. III – 39, 40, 41, 43. Chapt. II – 55.

First annihilate *Asakti*, then the *Kamana* (longing) will die by itself. Eventually preference also will be destroyed. When the attraction towards external objects ceases, then there yet remains *Trishna* (thirsting for objects). This is the most dangerous enemy of devotion. When the attraction towards objects, external as well as internal, ceases without any veil, then it is termed *Mukta* (freed) *Trishna*. The mere thought of longing that such and such a thing should come to oneself is *Trishna*. It is this strong chain of *Trishna* that you should unshackle yourself from, if you want to grow in *Bhakti*. Cut off the *Trishna-tantu* (the thread of sense-hankering) by the sword of *Vairagya*. This is *"Nirodha"* or control of desire.

## निरोधस्तु लोकवेदव्यापारन्यासः ॥८॥

**Sutra 8. Nirodhastu lokavedavyaparanyasah.**

*On the contrary, control of desires means the resignation to the Lord of all worldly and scriptural activities.*

निरोधः Nirodha: inhibition of desires; तु tu: on the contrary; लोकवेदव्यापारस्य Lokavedavyaparasya: of worldly and scriptural activities; न्यासः Nyasah: resignation or consecration (to the Supreme).

Control of desires does not mean intense fight with desires. The more you fight with desires, the stronger and more intense they will become. Do not add further fuel to the fire of desire. Reduce your activities. Cultivate dispassion. Learn to discriminate. Pray. Sing. Do Japa. The desires will gradually lose very much of their force.

When divine love grows, renunciation of action comes by itself. The devotee is God-intoxicated. He knows nothing but his beloved Lord. His mind is ever fixed on the form of his Lord. He is not capable of doing any action enjoined by the Smritis or the Vedas. All activities leave him of their own accord.

He sees nothing else but God. He speaks of nothing else but God. He does not listen to anything. He has no craving or desire. Sometimes his voice is choked. He sits silently. How can he work at this stage?

**Nirodha:** The word Nirodha is not used here in the ordinary way as "restraint". It is used in a special sense, viz., *Nyasa* or 'renunciation', or 'dedication'.

**Loka Veda Vyapara:** Renunciation of worldly activities and scriptural duties does not mean here the abandoning of such activities themselves, but the effacement of egoism, selfishness, attachment – to fruits, craving, etc. The activities cannot be stopped. They can be consecrated or dedicated to the Lord by complete surrender of the individual soul to the Lord.

Even the distinction of sacred and secular (worldly) duty vanishes for a realised devotee. Every work is sacred to him. Every work is a sacred offering unto the Lord. Every work is an expression of his love for God.

Complete surrender of one's will to the Lord leads to Samadhi or union with the Lord.

A worldly-minded man cannot work without expectation of fruits of his works. He reaps the fruits by going to heaven. He comes back again to this Mrityuloka when the virtuous works are exhausted. He again does good and evil Karmas. Thus he is caught up in the never ending wheel of Samsara or Avagamana-Chakra. Rishis, seers and the Vedas, therefore, advise that the works should be performed without expectation of fruits and should be consecrated to the Lord as Isvararpana. Then the heart is purified and Bhakti develops. That is the reason why Lord Krishna advises Arjuna: "Whatever thou doest, whatever thou eatest, whatever thou offerest, whatsoever thou givest, whatsoever thou doest of austerity O Kaunteya! do thou that as an offering unto Me." Ch. IX – 27. Patanjali Maharshi, the exponent of Raja Yoga philosophy, also says: "*Ishvarapranidhanadva*". "Success is speedy in Yogic practice and attainment of Samadhi by surrendering the fruits of works at the feet of the Lord as an offering." *Ishvara Pranidhana* is an important item in his Kriya-Yoga and Niyama.

Egoism, ambition and Vasanas are obstacles in the

way of self-surrender. Subtle hidden Vasanas will try to come to the surface of the mind. Desire which is suppressed for some time will again manifest with re-doubled force, if the aspirant is not careful, if there is some waning in his Vairagya and spiritual practice, and if he mixes with worldly-minded people. Generally, the aspirant consciously or unconsciously, wittingly or unwittingly keeps up some desires for his gratification. He does not wish to part completely with his desires. Therefore, the self-surrender does not become perfect and unreserved. So the grace of the Lord does not descend. Even if there is an atom of desire or egoism, there is no possibility of Divine Grace. Mira says, "I have given up my mind, my heart, my soul, my Chitta, my intellect, my all to my beloved Giridhar Gopal." This is complete self-surrender. Mark the words "my all." The Lord becomes a slave of a Bhakta only when he has made absolute, ungrudging, self-surrender. He is very cruel and puts His devotee to severe tests and trials. Only when Surdas poked his eyes with the thorns and remained without food and water in the thick jungle, Lord Krishna appeared before him with sweetmeats and water. He did not hear the words of Draupadi so long as she kept up her own strength and traces of egoism. When she cried aloud with perfect sincerity and total resignation: "O Dvarakanath, my beloved! Come to my rescue." Then He ran to the scene and she had abundant cloth and her modesty was saved. Nyasa means renunciation. This brings Nirodha (control) of mind. It is renunciation of the fruits of works. Renunciation of egoism is Sarva Tyaga (renunciation of all). All desires, selfishness, Raga-dvesha, body-idea, Deha-abhimana, are hanging on egoism. Egoism is the pivot on which all these are centred. Kill egoism. Then the surrender becomes complete. Even if there is a tinge or grain of egoism, the Lord will not reveal Himself.

## तस्मिन्ननन्यता तद्विरोधिषूदासीनता च ॥९॥

**Sutra 9. Tasminnananyata tadvirodhishudasinatha cha.**

*(Nirodha also means) single-minded devotion to the Lord and indifference to all that is antagonistic to Him.*

तस्मिन् Tasmin: in Him, in that; अनन्यता Ananyata: single-heartedness, identification, complete unification; तद्विरोधिषु Tadvirodhishu: in respect of what is opposed to it; उदासीनता Udasinata: indifference; च cha: and.

**Ananyata:** Single-mindedness is an important factor in devotion.

Surrender everything to the Lord. Do every action as an offering unto the Lord. Practise absolute surrender to the Lord.

When you surrender your mind, ego, body, to the Lord you will realise your oneness with the Lord.

A devotee realises that the Lord alone is acting through him, that the Lord alone has given him intelligence and opportunities, etc. He does not take any credit for himself. He attributes everything to Lord's grace.

A worldy man forgets all these and allows his ego assert itself at every step.

Your real enemy is your ego. Slay this ego, the enemy of devotion and peace. Be indifferent to its persuasions and promptings. Place it as an offering at the lotus feet of the Lord. This is the real flower that can be offered to the Lord.

The child thinks of the mother and mother alone. A passionate husband thinks of his wife and wife alone. A greedy man thinks of his money and money alone. Even so the devotee should entertain in his heart the picture of his Ishtam and Ishtam alone. Then he can have Darshan of God easily. Lord Krishan says to Arjuna, "He who constantly thinketh upon Me, not thinking ever of another, by him I am easily reached, O Partha, by this ever-harmonised Yogi." Chapt. VIII-14.

The single-minded devotion can only manifest by constant and protracted practice in a quiet room and Vairagya. Whenever the wavering and unsteady mind runs out, curb it, draw it and fix it again and again at the face or lotus feet of the Lord. It takes some time for the collection of the scattered rays of the mind and for establishing new habits in the mind. One should not be discouraged in the beginning. Patience, perseverance, attention, faith, strong will, fortitude, power of endurance are needed. These virtues should be cultivated. Satsanga, dietetic adjustment, milk and fruits, fasting, control of sleep, reduction in the hours of sleep, sometimes seclusion, observance of Mouna, Brahmacharya should be resorted to. The mind is naturally prone to love of ease, gluttony, laziness, seeking of comforts, gossiping, worldly talks, sight-seeing, etc. It should be gradually trained, tamed and disciplined by suitable methods. It is like a spoiled, indulgent child. It must be sometimes coaxed, while at other times, if it is unruly and disobedient, it must be threatened and whipped. Fasting is whipping. Mouna is whipping.

*Udaseenata* is indifference to sensual enjoyments and sensual objects. Objects are enemies of God. Sons, wife, property, cattle, house, friends, relatives are the enemies of God. You must cherish perfect indifference to those objects. You must destroy ruthlessly *Moha* for these objects and develop the state of *Nirabhimanata* (without 'mineness'). *Moha* is infatuated love towards body, children, father, mother and wife. Attachment to the body is deep-rooted. You must not think of body, and its wants too

much. Thoughts of body, thoughts of food, thoughts of wife
and children make you forget God. You cannot have
thoughts of God if you have thoughts of Anatma things
(non-sentient objects).

There is supreme joy and bliss in *Udaseenata*. You will
find in Mundaka Upanishad, "Two birds, inseparable companions, dwell upon one and the same tree. One of them
eats the sweet fruit, the other looks on without eating. On
the same tree, the Jiva, immersed in worldliness and bewildered, grieves on account of helplessness. But when he
sees the other, the Lord, who is adored by all and His
glory, then his grief passes away." Here one bird is the Jiva,
the other bird is the Lord. The tree is this body.
*Udaseenata* destroys all sorts of attachments and desires.
Attachment is death. *Udaseenata* is eternal life. Lord
Krishna says, "An *Udaseen* (indifferent man) is dear to
me." Chapt. XII – 16. Just as the spectators of a cricket or
foot-ball match enjoy the game nicely, so also an *Udaseena*
who is quite unconcerned with the world enjoys as a witness of this world-dharma and passes beyond grief. In the
Gita you will find: "Unattachment, absence of self-iden-
tification with son, wife or home and constant balance of
mind in wished for and unwished for events" – This is
declared to be the Wisdom. Chapt. XIII – 11.

Remember dear readers! That *Udaseenata* is not
physical nudity or inaction. It is not the living on neem
leaves or cow's dung or groundnut. Performance of foolish
kinds of austerities (Mudha tapas) does not constitute
*Udaseenata*. Lord Krishna says, "the men who perform
severe austerities, unenjoined by the scripture, wedded to
vanity and egoism, impelled by the force of their desire
and passion, unintelligent, tormenting the aggregated ele-
ments forming the body and Me also, seated in the inner

body, know these to be demoniacal in their resolves."
Chapt. XVIII—5, 6.

*Udaseenata* is purely a mental state. Queen Chudalai
was a perfect *Udaseena*, though she reigned a dominion,
but her husband Sikhidwaja was attached to his begging
bowl and walking stick though he lived in a forest. A man
may be attached to his kowpeen or a fountain-pen even,
whereas a king like Janaka may be a perfect *Udaseena*
though he is amidst luxuries and opulence. Worldly people
attach much importance to external show only. This is a
great pity. This is their horrible mistake. A man may be
nude and yet his mind may be full of desires. Some
hypocrites pretend to be Virakta Sadhus to exploit the
householders. Householders should use their discrimination always *Udaseenata Vritti* comes from *Mithya Drishti*
and *Dosha Drishti* in objects and from discrimination between the real and the unreal.

## अन्याश्रयाणां त्यागोऽनन्यता ॥१०॥

**Sutra 10. Anyasrayanam tyagonanyata.**

*Unification or exclusive devotion or single heartedness
means the giving up of all supports.*

अन्याश्रयाणां Anyasrayanam: of all other supports; त्यागः
tyagaha: renunciation, giving up; अनन्यता ananyata: unification, single-heartedness.

The cultivation of devotion may be disturbed by
various influences in the daily life. Desires and cravings
will continue to trouble the aspirant. The devotee should
not seek the help of instruments other than those
employed in the cultivation of devotion, namely listening
to talks about the Lord, singing His name, etc.

The devotee knows no one else than his Beloved

Lord. The Lord is all in all for him. The Lord is the sole refuge for him. He lives for the Lord and Lord alone. He works for Him alone.

The Lord is his own support, his only strength, his only hope and his only object of faith. Just as the eyes of the Chatak bird are fixed on the cloud, so also his eyes are fixed on his Beloved Lord alone.

The devotee does not conceive the existence of any object other than his Beloved Lord. How then will he seek the shelter of any other person or object. He sees nothing else besides the Lord.

All objects in this world are perishable. Nothing other than God can protect one from the troubles of this world. Therefore, the devotee abandons everything in this world and depends upon God and God alone, who is eternal, who is omnipotent, and who is all merciful.

To the chaste and devoted wife, no male except her Lord exists even in dream. Even so for a sincere devotee no object or person except his beloved Lord exists even in dream. He is absorbed in the Lord, the object of his love and devotion.

Here is a definition of *ananyata*: mind is clinging to persons, objects or places with leech-like tenacity. Wherever there is a little sensual pleasure, the mind is attached there, through Raga. All the pleasure centres should be destroyed. Then alone the mind can be turned towards God with one-pointed concentration. The mind is always jumping like a monkey. Now it thinks of sweetmeats or fruits. Then it wants to talk something with some friends. Just as a Chinese is drawn hither and thither by his five wives, so also the mind is tossed hither and thither by the five Indriyas. It is always restless.

Through *Vairagya* and discrimination all these

pleasure-centres should be destroyed. Then through constant, steady Abhyasa of Japa-dhyana, it should be turned
towards God. The struggle is doubtless keen and hard.
How difficult it will be to send up the waters of the Ganga
above towards 'Badri-Narayan'! Still more difficult it will
be for taking the mental energy towards God. It is easy to
direct the mental energy towards sensual objects. It is but
natural. It is the nature of the mind to run by itself towards
objects without the least exertion. It is its *Swabhava*. Lord
Krishna says:

*Abhyasa Yoga Yuktena chetasa nanya gaamina,*
*Paramam purusham divyam yati parthanuchintayan.*

"With the mind not wandering after anything else,
harmonised by continued practice, constantly meditating,
O Partha, one goeth to the Spirit Supreme Divine." Ch.
VIII — 8. "Place thy mind in Me, into Me let thy reason
enter; then without doubt thou shalt abide in Me hereafter.
But if thou art not able firmly to fix thy mind on Me then
by the Yoga of practice (Abhyasa Yoga) seek to reach Me,
O Dhananjaya." Chapter XII — 8, 9. In the practice of concentration one should have the same patience and perseverance as that of the bird which tried to empty the
ocean with its beak or blade of grass. Arjuna aimed at the
bird above by seeing the reflection of the bird in the water.
The arrow-maker was so much absorbed in his work that
he did not notice the huge crowd of Raja and his retinue.
Such must be the nature of concentration in God in the
Adhyatmic battlefield. Just as the bird that is tied to a post
flutters about hither and thither and eventually rests on the
post, so also the mind that wanders about here and there
in sensual objects finally rests in God, through the practice
of one-pointed concentration and devotion.

# लोकवेदेषु तदनुकूलाचरणं तद्विरोधिषूदासीनता ॥ ११ ॥

Sutra 11. Lokavedeshu tadanukulacharanam tadvirodhishudasinata.

*By "indifference to all which are hostile to Him" is understood the performance of these secular and religious activities which are congenial to Him.*

लोक वेदेषु Lokavedeshu: regarding secular and religious activities; तदनुकूलाचरणं Tadanukula acharanam: practices or performances which are congenial to Him; तद्विरोधिषूदासीनता Tadvirodhishudasinata: indifference to all which are hostile to Him.

In the eighth aphorism we have been taught to direct all our energies of thought and action towards God. Now we are again enjoined to respect to some extent the dictates of religion and morality. Here seems, therefore, to arise some confusion. This is only superficial. Only selfish activities must be given up, in order to get rid of desires. All works which can help to cultivate devotion must be regularly practised. There must be active co-operation with the divine plan. This Sutra explains the indifference to obstacles of Bhakti referred to in Sutra 9.

You must have faith in the existence of God when you perform sacrifices, penances and charity. You must do all actions for His sake. Then alone it is beneficial. Then alone it will endure.

The Gita, Bhagavatam and all sacred scriptures are guides to the conduct of a devotee. The teacher will interpret the sacred scriptures and guide the devotees.

A devotee does not do any action which is not pleasing to God, which does not help in the growth of devotion, which goes against the will of his Lord.

Prahlada renounced his atheistic father; Vibheeshana,

his Asuric brother; Bharata, his cruel mother; Bali, his preceptor even; the Gopis of Vraj, their husbands. But they all contributed to the welfare of the world. They are all regarded as benefactors of the world.

The devotee does all actions which are pleasing to the Lord till he attains God-realisation. He abandons activities that are prohibited by the scriptures such as theft, adultery, taking animal food and liquor. He abandons all selfish actions. But he does *Nitya* (obligatory) and *Naimittika* (incidental) in strict conformity with the procedure laid down in the Vedas without any expectation of fruits.

Lord Krishna says: "If also thou art not equal to constant practice, be intent on My service; performing actions for My sake, thou shalt attain perfection." Ch. XII – 12. "Acts of sacrifice, gift and charity should not be relinquished, but should be performed; sacrifice, gift and also austerity are the purifiers of the intelligent." Ch. XVIII – 5.

These rituals purify the heart and prepare the ground of Antahkarana for the growth of devotion. These actions should be performed without attachment and without expectation of fruit. The sacrifice which is offered by men without desire for fruit as enjoined by the ordinances, under the firm belief that sacrifice is a duty, is pure. The three kinds of austerities, viz., physical, verbal and mental Tapas prescribed in the seventeenth chapter of the Gita purify the heart rapidly. They are: –

1. Physical:

Devadvijaguru prajna pujanam sauchamarjavam Brahmacharyamahimsa cha sariram tapa uchyate.

Worship given to the Gods, to the twice-born, to the teachers and to the wise, purity, straight-forwardness, continence and harmlessness are called the austerity of the body.

2. Verbal:

Anudvegakaram vakyam satyam priyahitam cha yat
svadhyayabhyasanam chaiva vangmayam tapa uchyate.

Speech causing no annoyance, truthful and beneficial,
the practice of the study of the scriptures are called the
austerity of speech.

3. Mental:

Manah prasada saumyatvam maunamatmavinigrahah
Bhavasamsuddivriyetat tapo manasamuchyate.

Serenity of mind, good heartedness, silence, self control, purity of nature are called the austerity of the mind.

This threefold austerity, performed by men with the
utmost faith, without desire for fruit, harmonised, is said
to be pure.

Without purification of the mind, there is no hope of
cultivating Bhakti in your heart.

Without purification of the mind, there is no hope of
cultivating Bhakti in your heart.

Agnihotra, Vaishvadev, Brahma Yajna, Sandhyavan-
danam in the three periods of time, Panch Maha Yajna —
all are best calculated to purify the Chitta.

They should be performed daily without any break.
Observance of *Chandrayana Vrita* and *Krichara Vrita*
destroys sins effectively. They serve the purpose of *Prayaschitta* for expiating sin. The more the mind-mirror is
cleaned the better it is. Though these ceremonies are not
necessary for an advanced Bhakta, they are very essential
for neophytes.

Sraaddha, Tarpan, observances and gifts on the occasions of eclipses should not be neglected. Consult the
code of Manu or Yajnavalkya Smriti and you will get
abundant information on this subject. Various kinds of

*Prayaschitta* destroy various kinds of sin. If you find it difficult to consult the scriptures, consult the Pundits and Acharyas and they will guide you. If you do not observe these rituals, you will be subject to *pratyavaya dosha*, the sin of omission. Jaimini lays great stress on Karmas (Aghihotra, etc).

*Pradosha Vrita, Ekadasi Vrita* are observances that propitiate Lord Siva and Lord Hari respectively. They should also be observed rigidly.

भवतु निश्चयदाढ्र्यादूर्ध्वं शास्त्ररक्षणम् ॥१२॥

### Sutra 12. Bhavatu nischayadadhyadurdhvam sastrarakshanam.

*Let a man protect the scriptural teachings even after his spiritual realisation becomes well established.*

भवतु Bhavatu : Let there be; निश्चयदाढ्र्यात् Nischaya dardhyat: after realisation becomes firmly established; ऊर्ध्वम् Urdhvam: after; शास्त्रलक्षणम् sastrarakshanam: protection of scriptural teachings.

Let there be strict adherence to the injunctions of the Sastras till a firm conviction in God is attained, also till profound devotion is fully developed. Actions enjoined by the scriptures should be diligently performed, till that state of absolute forgetfulness of external existence is reached.

Even after firm establishment in divine resolve the scriptures must be respected. The scriptures are the words of God. They are guiding lights for the aspirants. Swerving even an inch from the path chalked out by the Sastras will bring about a downfall for the devotees.

Some aspirants foolishly imagine that they have attained perfection and that they are above the laws of scriptures. They do not observe the laws. They break them. They are deluded souls. They will get hopeless downfall.

The personal example of a devotee verily exercises a tremendous influence over others.

The devotee must be steady. He must have first intellectual conviction and then firmness in living up to the ideal. He must practise the principles. He must live up to the principles which he knows by conviction are essential for his happiness, spiritual evolution and God-realisation.

**Sastra Rakshanam:** When one is established in Dharma he is eligible to protect the Sastras. He is now able to defend the Sastras against attacks.

Others can protect the Sastras by living up to the ideas of the Sastras. This is also Sastra Rakshanam or protection of Sastras and Dharma.

Men of realisation should follow the scriptures in their actual life. They should set an example by their own life and teachings. Only then can the ordinary man adopt them for guidance in his life.

Lord Krishna says in the Gita, "But the ignorant, faithless, doubting self goeth to destruction, neither this world, nor that beyond, nor happiness, is there for the doubting self." (IV-40). "Therefore let the scriptures be thy authority, in determining what ought to be done or what ought not to be done. Knowing what has been declared by the ordinances of the scriptures, thou oughtest to work in this world." (XVI-24).

The mind should not be allowed to have its own ways. He who follows the injunctions of the Sastras will evolve quickly. He will have no uneasiness in mind. He will be cheerful and fearless. He will have satisfaction. He will feel that he is on the right path and progressing rapidly in spirituality. He will feel the nearness of God. He will have peace of mind.

Scriptures are infallible. Vedas have come out from the mouth of God. They are revelations. They are traditionally handed down from Rishis and seers to their disciples in succession (Parampara). So long as there is world, there are scriptures and teachers to guide the people in the path of Truth and Righteousness. The number of teachers my be few in the iron age but they do exist. Books are not eternal. But the ideas in the Vedas are eternal.

It does not require much wisdom and reasoning to have a firm conviction in the existence of God. I do not know why these rationalists, socialists and materialistic scientists are unnecessarily racking their brains, fighting and doubting. It is really a great pity! It is their stiff egoism that makes them deny the existence of God. Whether they accept His existence or not, He is shining from eternity to eternity. The sun is always there whether the owls accept the existence of the sun or not. There are gross impurities in their minds which screen and cloud their understanding. There are sins in their *Antahkarana* which make their intellects perverted. They will have to wait for some time for grasping.

Just as a young plant is fenced in the beginning and protected, so also a neophyte in the path of devotion should be well protected. If he mixes with atheists, he will lose his faith in God quickly. He must be always in the company of Sadhus, Mahatmas and Bhaktas. Their company is an iron fortress for him. If the injunctions of the Sastras are rigidly followed nothing can shake one's convictions. Just as a nail is driven deep into a plank by frequent hammering so also the Samskaras and convictions become very deep by observing strictly the sacred laws of the scriptures. This is the meaning of this Sutra.

## अन्यथा पातित्याशंकया ॥१३॥

**Sutra. 13. Anyatha patitya sankaya.**

*For, otherwise there is the risk of a fall.*

अन्यथा Anyatha: otherwise; पातित्याशंकया Patitya Sankaya : risk of a fall.

If the devotee who has made some spiritual progress is not careful, if he is not observing the rules of the scriptures, he may easily relapse into past habits.

He who deliberately violates the rules of good conduct prescribed by the scriptures will surely have a downfall. He will return to his previous state of worldliness and ignorance.

"He who ignores the injunctions of the scriptures and follows the promptings of desires can neither attain perfection, nor happiness, nor the supreme state." Gita XVI-23.

What may have been useful in the past may not be useful in course of time, under other circumstances and surroundings. There arises necessities for many readjustments in the scriptures. Realised persons should test the scriptures in the light of their own spiritual experiences. They should prune away superfluities and excrescences and remould if necessary the rules to suit the capacity of the people. Then alone the scriptures will be protected (Sastra Rakshanam).

Maya is very powerful. Mysterious is the power of Moha and desire! That is the reason why Lord Krishna says: "O son of Kunti, the excited senses of even a wise man, though he be striving, impetuously carry away his mind. Such of the roving senses as the mind yieldeth to, that hurries away the understanding, just as the gale hurries away a ship upon the waters." Chapt.II-60, 67.

You are all aware how the Rishi Visvamitra of great Tapas became a victim to the influence of the celestial nymph. Even Lord Buddha had to face Mara. This world is full of temptations. There is fear of fall at every moment. A beginner, a Tyro, is unable to resist temptations. He falls a prey to its influence quite readily. The Sadhaka must be very, very careful. He should observe the injunctions of the Sastras. They pave a long way in keeping him from falling. He should not test his spiritual strength at the very outset when he had made a little progress only. Reaction may set in. The Indriyas will revolt. The mind will become furious. He will become a victim to passion. Even at the present moment, such instances of Yoga-bhrashtas are not lacking. When one is put to test he fails. Jaimini was tried by his Guru, Sri Vedavyasa. He failed in his Brahmacharya. Physical control alone will not suffice. No evil thoughts should arise in the mind. There must not be any unholy thrill or unholy vibration in the mind, even. This is the highest standard to purity. The Gita says, "Who sitteth, controlling the organs of action, but dwelling in his mind on the objects of the senses, that bewildered man is called a hypocrite." Cha. III-6.

Some foolish young Sadhakas do some Sadhana for four or five years in Himalayan caves, see some dazzling lights during meditation, hear some *anahat* sounds in the ears and think they are realised souls. They enter the world quickly for preaching, and mix with the house-holders freely and get a hopeless downfall rapidly. What you have gained by rigid Sadhana in twelve years will be lost in twelve seconds if you mix promiscuously with house-holders and if you do not take proper precautions. You should never come out to the plains till you attain Brahma or Brahma-Sthiti, till you become a full-blown Yogi or Jnani.

Therefore adhere to the injunctions of the Sastras till you develop supreme devotion. The observances will drop by themselves when you are established in highest devotion.

लोकोऽपि तावदेव किन्तु भोजनादिव्यापारस्त्वाशारीर-
धारणावधि ॥१४॥

**Sutra 14. Lokopi tavadeva kintu bhojanadi vyaparastv-asariradharanavadhi.**

*Social customs and practices also may be followed in like manner, to the same extent only (as scriptural injunctions). But eating, drinking, dressing should be continued as long as one wears this body.*

लोका Lokah: social practices, social customs and usages; अपि Api: also; तावद् tavad; that much, to that extent; एव Eva: only; किन्तु kintu. But; भोजनादि-व्यापार Bhojanadivyaparah: activities such as eating (drinking, dressing, sleep, exercise); तु tu: but, on the other hand; आशरीरधारणावधि a-sarira-dharanavadhi: as long as one wears this body.

Worldly duties such as one's occupation in life, and maintaining the family, etc., should also be carefully and scrupulously performed along with religious duties according to the injunctions of the scriptures. A time will come when all activities, religious as well as mundane, will drop by themselves.

Tavadeva: (that much).

Sarira Dharana: This means not mere existence but preservation of health. One cannot serve God and humanity without good health.

The extent to which the devotee may take liberties

with existing rules, as far as necessary for saving the society (Lokarakshnam).

He will have to conform to those social rules which are essential for the preservation of the safety of the society.

The customary injunctions also should be followed like the scriptural injunctions. They are also helpful to the aspirant in the beginning. When he is fully established in supreme devotion and piety, he can safely dispense with the scriptural as well as customary injunctions. They will drop themselves when he advances in purity and devotion. But on the contrary, eating and drinking will continue as long as he lives.

# DIFFERENT DEFINITIONS OF BHAKTI

## तल्लक्षणानि वाच्यन्ते नानामतभेदात् ॥१५॥

**Sutra 15. Tallakshanani vachyante nanamatabhedat.**

*The characteristics of Bhakti are described variously on account of difference in view-points (according to the different schools).*

तल्लक्षणानि Tallakshanani: its characteristic marks or indications of devotion; वाच्यन्ते Vachyante: are being described or stated; नानामतभेदात् Nanamatabhedat: according to diverse opinions or owing to difference in view points.

Thinkers agree as to the essential character of devotion; but they give prominence to one or other of its various manifestations in order to indicate its nature from their several points of view.

Different teachers have defined Bhakti in different ways. After giving their views first, Devarishi Narada advances his own views in the matter.

**Lakshanani:** marks.

The inner experiences of Bhakti is purely subjective. The mental condition of a devotee is known only to himself. But the devotees conduct themselves in different ways. We can recognise the characteristics or marks of devotion. Every change in the heart finds external manifestation in the behaviour as well as the appearance of the devotee.

In this and the succeeding nine Sutras Narada gives a

description of Bhakti as given by some writers who have preceded him and shows how his own view is more complete than that of any of his predecessors.

No two minds are constituted exactly alike and so there is room for difference of opinion and variety in the description of the same experiences. Differences in description do not point to differences in the experiences itself.

Now let us examine the experiences expressed about Bhakti by some well known saints. In the Sivanandalahari, Sri Sankara speaks of Bhakti as the sticking of thoughts to the feet of the Lord permanently, just as a needle sticks to the magnet, the seed to the Ankola tree, a virtuous wife to her husband or a creeper to a tree.

In Devi Bhagavatam, supreme love is compared to oil poured from one vessel to another (Tailadharavat). There should not be any break in the regular succession of thoughts about God.

In Bhagavatam, Maitreya says that Bhakti is a natural settlement of the mind upon the highest truth from which all objects and senses have come out.

Kapila described it as a flow of uninterrupted thoughts towards God seated in the hearts of all beings like the flow of waters of the Ganga towards the sea.

Prahlada prays that the love which the worldly people have for the objects be turned into Bhakti by being directed towards God.

In the Narada Panchatantra, Bhakti is spoken of as service rendered to the Lord of the senses through the senses without being clouded by *Upadhis* and purified by being directed towards Him.

Sri Ramanujacharya identifies Bhakti with loving meditation.

Sandilya describes Bhakti as supreme love of God. Svapnesvara comments on this Sutra and says that this love results from the realisation of the greatness of the Lord. Thus there are different views. These views are different on account of the differences in which the divine love is experienced by devotees who are in different stages of development or evolution and also in different moods or states.

Lakshana means mark or characteristic or sign. All devotees unanimously agree in the essential characteristics of devotion. But some give prominence to certain indications; while others to certain other marks. That is all. There cannot be any fundamental difference in the essence.

*Nanamatabhedat* means according to various opinions.

पूजादिष्वनुराग इति पाराशर्यः ॥१६॥

**Sutra 16. Pujadishvanuraga iti parasaryah.**

*Vyasa, the son of Parasara, is of opinion that Bhakti consists in attachment to worship of God and other similar acts.*

पूजादिषु Pujadishu: in worship and like performances; अनुराग Anuraga: devotion, attachment, ardour; इति iti: thus; पाराशर्य Parasarya son of the sage Parasara.

Ardour in worship and similar performances is the chief characteristic of the love of God or the mark of devotion according to sage, Sri Vyasa.

Worship ranges from the worship of an image as a symbol of God to the worship of Virat, Hiranyagarbha, etc.

Worship should be both external and internal or mental (Manasic Pooja).

When the devotee develops attachment for worship of God, his mind will automatically withdraw itself from the objects of the world.

Those who perform worship of God attain the Supreme eternal and blissful abode of God.

The devotee establishes identity with the Absolute through rigorous and constant meditation. This is the highest form of worship.

The worship is offered to the Lord within us. This is also internal worship. Internal worship or Manasic Pooja is more powerful than the external worship with flowers, etc. Bheema did Manasic pooja. It was more powerful than the external worship done by Arjuna.

Poosalan Nayanar, one of the Tamil saints out of the sixty-three Tamil Saints who are adored in all Siva temples, mentally constructed a temple for Siva in his village, Tiruninravur. It took for him three years to construct the temple mentally. He fixed also mentally the date on which the Kumbhabhishekam ceremony was to be conducted. Lord Siva attended the ceremony.

External Pooja consists of sixteen parts, viz., *Avahanam*, (invitation of the Lord); *Asanam* (offering of seat); *Padyam* (offering of water to wash the feet); *Arghyam* (offering of water as a mark of respect); *Achamanam* (water to be sipped); *Madhuparkam* (offering of milk and fruit); *Snanam* (bath); *Vastram* (offering of Clothes); *Yajnopaveetam* (putting sacred thread): *Gandham* and *Akshata* (offering of sandal paste and rice); *Pushpam* (offering of flowers); *Dhupam* (offering of incense); *Deepam* (waving of lights); *Neivedyam* (offering of food); *Tambulam* (offering beetles) and *Niranjanam* (the waving of lighted camphor).

**Pujadishu:** This refers to celebration of festivals, building and renovation of temples; sacred dance; devotional works of art such as painting and sculpture; acts of charity; digging of tanks; making of images, Vahanams or vehicles; lighting lamps; the daily supply of flowers, sandal paste, incense, scents, Bhog or Neivedya; giving of silks and clothes for the images and for decoration; etc.

Worship may be continued even after realisation. Sankara, Ramanuja, Madhva, Gauranga engaged themselves in worship even after realisation.

**Anuraga:** Anuraga means 'intense attachment to the Lord'. The word 'anuraga' ordianrily means only mere love but in Bhakti scriptures it means the love that arises out of the recognition of the divinity and splendour of God after realisation.

Prahlada says, "O Hari! May not the ceaseless flow of love and attachment leave my heart, while I am constantly meditating upon Thee." (Vishnu Purana – 1.20.19). Devotion cometh and goeth in the beginning. When it is fully ripe, the devotee has intense attachment to the lotus feet of the Lord. Even for the infinitesimal part of a second his mind does not stir from the point or Lakshya. This is Anuraga.

कथादिष्विति गर्गः ॥१७॥

**Sutra 17. Kathadishviti Gargah.**

*The sage Garga thinks that Bhakti consists in talks of His glory and greatness and the stories of His various sports and the like.*

कथादिषु Katha-adishu: in holy talks (of Lord's glory

and greatness) and the like (Anuraga : devotion) ; इति iti : thus; गर्ग Gargah: sage Garga (manyati-thinks).

Garga, an apostle of Bhakti, thinks that indulgence in talks of Lord's glory and greatness, fondness for spiritual conversation and the like is the sign of devotion or the characteristic of divine love.

The stories of the incarnations of God are most elevating, inspiring and soul-stirring. They instill devotion in the hearts of the hearers. There is a mysterious and marvellous charm in the stories pertaining to Avataras. A sincere devotee loses himself in the stories of Lord Rama or Lord Krishna.

Hearing the stories of the Lord removes the impurities of the mind and leads to God-realisation ultimately.

**Kathadishu:** Narration is *Katha*. "Adi" here includes also reading of the stories *"Patha"*, *Kirtan* (individual), *Sankirtan* (collective with musical instruments), *Japa* (prayer) *Harikathas* (discourses on spiritual topics), hymns, *Bhajans* or songs, theological literature.

Lord Krishna says in the Gita, "With their hearts fixed on Me and their life absorbed in Me, constantly discoursing and conversing with one another about Me, they are contented, and they rejoice. (Chapter X. 9).

Narada always goes about singing the glories of the Lord in ecstasy. Gauranga immersed himself in Sankirtan.

Parikshit delighted himself in listening to the glories of the Lord by Sir Suka.

Sri Suka says in Bhagavat, "Enquiring about Lord Krishna's stories purifies him who describes Him, him who enquires and him who listens."

Here is a difference of opinion. It is the hearing of

praises and greatness of the Lord that inspires a man to take to the spiritual path. Parikshit realised God through hearing from the sacred mouth of Sri Sukadev. Man gets several knocks and blows in the daily battle of life. He gets failures and disappointments. This world becomes a hot furnace to him. He approaches the Bhagavatas and hears the praises of God. Then the mind gradually is turned towards God. The mind of the rogue Ratnakar who turned towards God after meeting Narada.

## आत्मरत्यविरोधेनेऽति शाण्डिल्य ॥१८॥

**Sutra 18. Atmaratyavirodheneti Sandilyah.**

*The sage Sandilya thinks that it must be without hindrance to the enjoyment of bliss in the Atman.*

आत्मरति अविरोधेन Atmarati-avirodhena: without hindrance to the enjoyment of bliss in the Atman; इति Iti: Thus; शाण्डिल्यः Sandilya: sage Sandilya ; (मन्यते Manyate: thinks).

The sage Sandilya holds that it must be without being opposed to the delight in the Atman.

Sandilya is of the opinion that "These are Bhakti insofar as they do not clash with the contemplation of the Self."

Whatever draws the mind away from God can never be favourable to the culture of devotion. On the contrary, everything which relates to God and holds Him constantly before your mind's eyes, strengthens and deepens the flow of devotion.

Delight in the actions of the Lord is a mark of devotion, if it does not interfere with the delight in the Lord Himself. The hearing or study of the Leelas or sports of the Avataras or divine incarnations produces a profound feeling of devotion. This delight comes from the spirit in man. The soul is exalted comes from the spirit in man. The soul is exalted during divine esctasy. It is a calm, subjective experience of the devotee. Mistake not emotion for devotion.

Bhakti is supreme attachment to God, which is not opposed to love or self or Atma. God Himself exists as the soul in every being. Devotion to the soul is devotion to God. Devotion is quest for supreme Atman according to a Vedantin. Sandilya identifies God with Atman.

Remember that the enjoyment of the objects is not opposed to the enjoyment of the real bliss in the Atman and that sensual pleasure is a reflection or infinitesimal part of the supreme bliss of Atman.

God is an embodiment of bliss. The devotee who always dewlls in God must enjoy the bliss of God. There is always divine aura and bloom in his face. The eyes sparkle and glitter with Divine effulgence. Those who surround the devotee experience the bliss, because he radiates joy all around (vide Sutra 6). If a devotee is always morose and unhappy, if his countenance is cheerless, if he is peevish, there is surely some error in his Sadhana. He is not enjoying the bliss of the Self. Ananda is a very important sign of devotion. It is a fundamental sign of a jivanmukta too.

नारदस्तु तदर्पिताखिलाचारता तद्विस्मरणे
परमव्याकुलतेति ॥१९॥

**Sutra 19. Naradastu tadarpitakhilacharata tadvismarane paramavyakulateti.**

*But Narada is of the opinion that the essential characteristics of Bhakti are the consecration of all observances and activities through complete self-surrender to the Lord and extreme anguish in the event of forgetting Him.*

नारदः Naradah : Devarshi Narada; तु Tu: however, in distinction from others; तदर्पिताखिलाचारता Tadarpit-akhilacharata: the state of one who has consecrated all observances and all activities to the Lord through self-surrender; तद्विस्मरणे Tadvismarane : In the event of forgetting Him; परम व्याकुलता Parama Vyakulata : extreme anguish; इति iti : thus.

Is such a climax ever attainable? Yes; certainly. It is not at all an impracticable ideal, because there are instances.

Narada has in the above three Sutras given us the ideas of Vyasa, Garga and Sandilya. In this Sutra he is giving his own opinion.

Sutra 16 refers to devotion in actions, 17 to devotion in speech, while 18 lays stress on devotion in mind. Devotion to God in thought, word and deed is very essential for a truly spiritual life. Narada says that there cannot be real devotion unless there is complete self-surrender in every aspect of our life.

When the devotee lives solely for his Lord then he is a real Bhakta. The devotee becomes extremely restless and miserable at the slightest lapse in the remembrance of God. This is the teaching of Narada.

It is this mental condition that truly represents supreme devotion or Para Bhakti. Complete self surrender is the prime characteristic of Bhakti.

Narada has no quarrel with the definitions of Bhakti given by Vyasa, Garga and Sandilya. It is certainly proper and necessary to worship God, to sing His praises and to love God as the soul of all. Narada's definition of Bhakti covers the definitions of Bhakti given by Vyasa, Garga and

Sandilya and is complete in every way. It is a comprehensive definition. It points out the very essence of Bhakti.

Tu: This is introduced to indicate the difference between the previous definition of Bhakti and what Narada says.

Pooja, narrations, etc., are all inferior to that kind of devotion which Narada describes in this Sutra. In Pooja and narrations the devotee does not surrender his all.

In self-surrender there is the effacement of the ego. Any selfless work performed without egoism, with the attitude of self-surrender has a real place in devotional or spiritual life. It is a real offering to the Lord. God is pleased immensely.

The devotee gets *parama-vyakulata* when he forgets his Beloved. Lord Gouranga, Mira and the Gopis of Brindavan exhibited this sign. This is Virahaagni (pain from separation of the Lord). This feeling can hardly be described in words. It has to be felt. It breaks the heart of the devotee. This Sutra does not in any way contradict Sutra 18. An advanced Bhakta who always rests in God has no Viraha. He is always in divine bliss.

अस्त्येवमेवम् ॥२०॥

**Sutra 20. Astyevamevam.**

*There are such and such instances. (Examples do exist of such perfect expression of Bhakti. So it is. So it is.)*

एवं एवम् Evam evam : such and such, thus and thus; Udaharanam : example) ; अस्ति Asti : exists, there is.

The next Sutra will illustrate the view of Narada.

Bhakti is exactly as described in the foregoing aphorism.

## यथा व्रजगोपिकानाम् ॥२१॥

**Sutra 21. Yatha vrajagopikanam.**

*As for instance, in the case of the cow-maids of Vraja or Brindawan.*

यथा Yatha: for instance; व्रजगोपिकानाम् Vrajagopikanam; in the case of the Gopis of Vraja : the cow-maids of Vraja or Brindavan.

In the context, read the chapters 29 and 30 of Srimad Bhagavatam.

Although there have been great devotees like Sri Suka, Uddhava, Valmiki and others, Narada mentions the illiterate women of Vraja, as examples of the highest devotion. They played with Sri Krishna and identified themselves with Him in complete devotion.

They cared not for family tradition, reputation and personal comfort in order to live in perfect devotion to Lord Krishna. They said, "Wherever we look, we find Shyama, in the dark rain cloud, in the black pupils of our eyes, in the dark Tamal tree leaves, in the blue waters of Jumna, in the blue sky, etc."

Pure, divine love definitely exercises a levelling influence. It removes all inequalities and brings the lover and the beloved on the same level. It results in the fusion of personalities.

The Gopis were the crest-jewels among the devotees of the Lord. The love of the Gopis to the Lord cannot be adequately described in words. They dedicated their bodies, minds, possessions, souls, and their all to the Lord. They always sang the Lord's glories with their voices choked with emotion.

Lord Krishna spoke to them, "You have cut all

domestic ties for my sake. I cannot repay the debt of yours by serving you even for the life time of a celestial being. Please relieve Me from this liability out of your own generosity."

The Lord says, "The Gopis have given themselves up to Me, their heart and soul. They think that I am their life. They have abandoned all their closest relatives for My sake. I ever support those who cast aside all worldly pleasures for My sake." Bhagavata Chapter X-46, verse 4.

The secret of Rasaleela can only be understood by pure souls who are free from passion. Persons with a pure heart can understand the pure divine love of Gopis. Gopis were exalted beings. They should not be judged by human standards.

The Vaishnava saints got their inspiration from this love of the Gopis. Nimbarka, Jayadeva, Gauranga and Vallabha founded their theology on this Brindavana-Lila.

Nammalvar, Sri Chaitanya, Jayadeva also were great devotees.

The Gopis surrendered all their actions at the lotus feet of Lord Krishna. They experienced acute agony if they missed His presence even for a moment. When they heard the sweet, melodious flute of their beloved they left their houses while milking the cows. With minds absorbed in Krishna they rushed forth to where their lover was without taking notice of each other. Some did not wait to see the boiling of the milk. Some did not take down boiled wheat from the oven. Some were serving their husbands and some were taking their own food. But they all left their work half-finished. They gave up their household duties, with clothes and ornaments all in disorder, they hurriedly went to Krishna. When Krishna disappeared they asked the trees if they had seen their lover. They enquired of the creepers, the earth and the deer.

तत्रापि न माहात्म्यज्ञानविस्मृत्यपवादः ॥२२॥

**Sutra 22. Tatrapi na mahatmyajnanavismrityapavadah.**

*Even there (the love of the Gopis), there is no particular reason for forgetting the glory and greatness of Lord.*

तत्र Tatra : there, i.e., in respect of the example of the Gopis; अपि Api : even ; न na : not; माहात्म्य ज्ञानविस्मृत्यपवादः Mahatmya-jnana-vismrita-apavadah : particular reason for forgetting the glory and greatness of the Lord.

A full and conscious realisation of the grandeur and majesty of God increases all the more His supreme importance as an object of admiration and adoration in the eye of the devotee. Without a clear consciousness of the majesty and grandeur of God, devotion cannot operate as a persistent factor of spiritual development.

The Gopis danced in the moonlight and played with Sri Krishna and yet they were not unconscious of His divinity, His Omniscience and Omnipotence even for a second. They recognised Him as the soul of the universe and also as their own Atma.

The Gopis surrendered themselves to Sri Krishna knowing Him to be God Himself and the embodiment of Satchidananda. They said to Lord Krishna, "You are the primal Purusha or Purushottama, the protector of the Devas. You are the witness of everything. You have taken an incarnation for the protection of the whole world."

The play of the Gopis is a lesson for the worldly minded persons whose hearts are filled with passion to rise above passion by listening to the divine and holy stories of

Lord Krishna and Gopis of Brindavan. These are allegories which contain profound spiritual truths.

The author of the stories which depict the Leelas of Lord Krishna is the holy sage Vyasa and the narrator is his son, Sri Suka Deva, the greatest sage and seer. Lord Krishna was a child. So there cannot be any tinge of unholiness in the Leelas, which is attributed by some ignorant, dull-witted, passionate, foolish, worldly-minded, sensuous, worthless persons, who are on a level with animals in deep carnal, brutal instincts.

The Rishis of Dandaka forest wanted to embrace Lord Rama. Lord Rama said, "You will be born as Gopis of Brindavan. You will embrace Lord Krishna who is no other than my own Self." This is the cause for Rasaleela.

"Tatra api. Even there." Even though the Gopis had physical attachment to Lord Krishna, the attachment was of the nature of supreme devotion. It was perfectly taintless too.

The Gopis were absolutely unselfish. They were not jealous. All the Gopis were united to please Lord Krishna by their service. If the love was of a selfish type, no Gopi would have tolerated Krishna's loving another Gopi.

The Gopis did not seek a human lover but the Lord Himself.

Why does a man undergo miseries and sufferings? Because he has forgotten God owing to the influence of Avidya or Maya. That devotee in whom there is descent of His grace can never forget Him even for a second. Try to remember the Lord along with every breath, inspiratory and expiratory. Keep the Gita always in your pocket and a Japa Maala on your neck. Repeat His name always. Be in the company of Bhaktas. Study the Bhagavata or the Ramayana or the Gita daily. Then you cannot forget Him.

Reduce your activities. Do *Satya-vyavahara*. Reduce your wants. Destroy the desires as they spirng up in the mind. Do not try to fulfil them. Increase your Japa on Sundays. Do *Anushtana* of 4 lakhs of Japa in Easter, summer and Christmas holidays. Do Akhanda Japa or Akhanda Path of Bhagavata or Akhanda Kirtan for seven days during Janmashtami. During these seven days live on milk and fruits and wear clothing washed by your own hands. Observe perfect Mouna and celibacy. All the members of the house should follow these rules strictly. Then there is no possibility of forgetting Him. The Lord is quite close to you. Your house will be turned into Vaikuntha. The Lord says: "O Narada, I dwell not in Vaikuntha, nor in the hearts of Yogis, but I dwell there where my Bhaktas sing My name — *na aham vasami vaikunthe yoginam hridaye nacha, mad bhakta yatra gayanti tatra tishthami Narada.*"

## तद्विहीनं जाराणामिव ॥२३॥

**Sutra 23. Tadvihinam jaranamiva.**

*A love without it (the sense of greatness of the object loved — "the Lord") is simply a passion of a woman towards her paramour.*

तद्विहीनं Tad-vihinam : deprived of that, bereft of the knowledge of that (glory of the Lord or divine greatness); जाराणाम् Jaranam : of couples or paramours indulging in base, unlawful passion: इव Iva : like.

"Tat" or 'it' means love.

Deprived of the sense of divine greatness, devotion is like the love of a woman towards her paramour which is constantly shifting from person to person in an indefinite manner, according as one appears more desirable than another.

The love of Gopis was saturated with the knowledge of the Divine glory. It was of a very pure nature. It was *Shuddha Prem*.

The relation of the Gopis with Sri Krishna is liable to be misunderstood as something physical by the sensually-minded. Narada warns the students of Bhakti against mistaking the highest form of Divine Love for base passion.

The Gopis were in a drunken state. They were God-intoxicated. They were unconscious of their earthly existence. They were drowned in the ocean of Divine Bliss. The mind and senses ceased functioning. The external objects did not produce any impression on their minds.

Divine Love is true and pure. All love other than that for God is unlawful. To love any creature as a creature and not as divinity embodied in it is unlawful. Impure selfish love taints the heart of man.

Passion is not love at all. It is an animal instinct. It is carnal love. It is of a beastly nature. It is shifting. If the wife loses her beauty on account of some incurable malady she gets a divorce and the husband marries another. This state of affairs is going on in the world. But Bhakti is *Suddha prem*. It is divine love. It is unchanging. The devotee cherishes always the sense of majesty and magnanimity of the Lord. His *Ishtam* is the Lord of his very breath (Prananath or Pranavallabha). It is this idea that keeps up his devotion, nourishes and strengthens it. If this idea of the sense of greatness of the Lord is lacking, then he has no devotion. His devotion is tantamount to the passion of a lustful husband and wife. There is no grandeur in his devotion. Remembrance of the tenth chapter of the Gita where all the Vibhutis of God are described will keep up the idea of the sense of greatness of God. Devotion is a sublime sacred sentiment. It elevates the soul immediately to lofty heights of divinity. When a man comes to realise the *Mahima* of the Lord, all worldly desires die and all attachment and ties are broken and the man is keen and eager to have *Darshan* of the Lord.

नास्त्येव तस्मिस्तत्सुखसुखित्वम् ॥२४॥

**Sutra 24. Nasthyeva tasminstatsukhasukhitvam.**

*There i.e., in that illicit love there can certainly never be happiness of the other.*

तस्मिन् Tasmin: in that (profane love), therein, in illicit love; तत् सुखसुखित्वम् Tat sukhasukhitvam: happiness in the happiness of the other; न na: not; अस्ति asti: is, exists; एव eva: certainly.

In that sort of love, there is no idea at all of one's feeling happy in the happiness of the other.

In the case of the Gopis, the Beloved was God Himself. There was no desire in them for physical contact. They tried to make Sri Krishna happy by offering their all to Him.

They derived immense happiness from this act of service. They had no idea of any sensual enjoyment. Sensuality is selfish passion. It seeks gratification through others, but pure, divine love seeks to make the Beloved happy and to derive happiness from the happiness of the latter. The desire for gratification of one's own senses is *Kama* or sensuality. The object of *kama* is self-gratification, while Prema or pure love has the happiness of Sri Krishna for its object. The Gopis did not care for their own happiness. The happiness of Sri Krishna is the purpose of all their activities. They renounced all comforts, all worldly duties, etc., in order to worship Sri Krishna and make Him happy. There was no trace of Kama or sensuality in the

Gopis. Their love was exceedingly pure, divine and transcendent.

They surrendered all their possessions to Sri Krishna. They offered their body, mind, intellect, wealth, youth and life itself. They were very restless if they forget Sri Krishna even for a second. They understood the supreme greatness and glory of Sri Krishna. They rejoiced in the happiness of Krishna. Their happiness depended only on His happiness. The exalted state of the Gopis is indescribable!

There is no element of sacrifice in illicit love. There is physical passion in this love. There is deep selfishness. The love is mercenary.

In divine love the devotee sacrifices everything unto the Lord. There is a sense of self-forgetfulness. There is no trace of selfishness. The devotee does not at all care for his own happiness. He is willing to court suffering in order to make his Beloved happy.

In mercenary love, there cannot be any real happiness between the two, the lover and beloved. If the husband is in a dying condition, the wife takes the bank pass book and walks to her mother's house quietly. If the husband loses his job for some time, the wife shows wry faces, speaks harsh words and does not serve him properly with any love. This is selfish love. There is no real affection from the core of the heart. So there are always quarrels, fighting and Asanti in the house. Husbands and wives are not really united. There is always a tug of war. They pull on anyhow, dragging a dreary, cheerless existence.

Even our sisters of ill-fame show for some time abundant love, sweet smile, and honeyed words towards their customers, so long as they can extract money. Can you call this love and real happiness? Just tell me frankly. There are cunningness, diplomacy, crookedness and hypocrisy here.

# SUPREMACY OF DEVOTION

## सा तु कर्मज्ञानयोगेभ्योऽप्यधिकतरा ॥२५॥

Sutra 25. Sa tu karmajnanayogebhyopyadhikatara.

*It (supreme devotion) is again higher than action, knowledge and Yoga.*

सा Sa: It; devotion, that Para Bhakti; तु tu: again; in distinction from others; कर्मज्ञानयोगेभ्यः Karma-yoga-jnana-yogebhya; than action. knowledge and Yoga; अपि api: even; अधिकतरा Adhikatara: superior, higher, greater.

In Sutras 25 to 33 Narada explains the greatness of Para Bhakti. He says that Karma, Jnana and Yoga are methods to achieve the result whereas Bhakti is the result itself.

Yogi is one who enters into a living communion with God and perfectly realises His immanence and activity everywhere in the world.

Unless one is blessed with love of the Lord, unless one's heart is purified by devotion, it is impossible to perform unselfish service.

Without real devotion one cannot know the nature of the Lord.

In the beginning you can do your duty to your own family or country. But your heart should expand. You should consider all mankind as your family, the whole world as your country, the whole world as your home and body.

Bhakti or devotion is an end in itself. In Jnana and Yoga there is the risk of a fall. In the path of devotion there is no risk as the devotee receives full support and help from God. Moreover the path of devotion is open to all alike, irrespective of caste, creed, sex or spiritual capacity.

Karma is the performance of religious rites and the strict adherence to one's duties as enjoined by the Dharma Sastras. It is the performance of Varnashrama Dharma. There are *Nitya Karmas* like *Sandhyavandan*, etc., and *Naimittika Karmas*, occasional rites and periodical performances. The heart is purified performing such Karmas unselfishly and divine light or wisdom dawns in a pure heart.

A Karma Yogi regards work as worship. It is duty for duty's sake. Selfless service through the renunciation of the fruits of one's acts is a means for attaining God. There is no bondage in selfless service.

A Karma Yogi should cultivate the virtues tolerance, adaptability, sympathy, mercy, equal vision, balance of mind, cosmic love, patience, humility, generosity, nobility, self-restraint, control of anger, non-violence, truthfulness, moderation in eating, drinking and sleeping, simple living and endurance. Then alone will he have perfect success in the practice of Karma Yoga.

Karma Yoga is the exercise of the will; Jnana Yoga is the exercise of the intellect and reason; Bhakti Yoga is the exercise of the emotion. Will consecrates all activities through complete surrender to God; the intellect realises the glory and majesty of the Lord; the emotion experiences the bliss of divine ecstasy.

Arjuna puts a question to the Lord; "Those devotees who, ever harmonised, worship Thee and those also who worship the indestructible, the Unmanifested, of these who is the more learned in Yoga?" Chapter XII-1. The Lord gives the answer: "They who with mind fixed on Me ever harmonised worship Me, with faith supreme endowed, they in my opinion are the best in Yoga." Then again He says: "The Yogi is greater than even the wise; the Yogi is greater than the men of action; therefore become thou a Yogi, O Arjuna." And among all Yogis, he who, full of faith, with the inner Self, abiding in Me, adoreth Me, he is considered by Me to be the most completely harmonised." Chapter VI—46-47. You will find in the eighth chapter, Sloka 22 of the Gita: unswerving devotion to Me alone within whom all beings dwell, by whom all this is pervaded." And again in chapter XI-54 you will find "But by single-minded devotion, can I thus be perceived, O Arjuna, and known and seen in essence and entered, O, Parantapa."

There is the keynote of devotion and surrender throughout the Gita. Bhakti Marga is easy for the vast majority of persons. God takes a form for helping the devotees. There are no pitfalls or snares in the path. The Lord is ever ready to guide the devotee. He actually takes him by His hands and embraces him in His sweet bosom of love. He showers His grace on the devotees, as soon as He finds out that they are sincere and earnest. Success is sure in this path. Bhakti Marga is the easiest, safest, surest and quickest way for attaining highest bliss or God realisation. That is the reason why Narada Rishi says, "Bhakti is greater then Karma, Jnana and Yoga.

"Those who mount dizzy heights by austere practices fancying themselves liberated but being really unenlightened, because lacking in devotion to Thee, O Lotus-eyed One! Fall into a chasm not having loved Thy feet. Never so, however, Thy own, O Madhava, stray away from the path, being tied to Thee by bonds of affection and guarded by Thee, they walk fearlessly in the spiritual path.

फलरूपत्वात् ॥२६॥

### Sutra 26. Phalarupatvat.

*Because of its being of the nature of the result or fruit of all these.*

फलरूपत्वात् Phalarupatvat: because of its being of the nature of the result or fruit of all these.

Devotion is not a means to an end. It is both a means as well as an end. It is the end or culmination of all Sadhanas or disciplines. The hidden God is made manifest through devotion. Then man realises his own divine nature.

Various disciplines such as practice of Yoga, religious rites, self-control, vows of various kinds, service of one's teacher, cultivation of divine virtues are described in the sacred scriptures but devotion to the Lord is the end of them all.

Jnana is the fruit of the practice of Sadhana Chatush-taya, the fourfold Sadhana and meditation. Purity of heart and the effacement of the ego is the result of the practice of Karma Yoga.

Kaivalya is the fruit of the practice of Raja Yoga. But Bhakti is itself of the nature of result. In the case of Bhakti we begin with Bhakti and end with Bhakti. Love or Bhakti has not come as a result of anything. It has not come to a devotee as a new thing. It is always there.

Jnana, Karma and Yoga are the paths which give you

the result in the form of Bhakti or supreme devotion to the Lord.

Para Bhakti is the goal itself. It is the highest stage. It is not fruit but it is of the nature of fruit. It is superior to other Yogas. The other Yogas represent a lower stage in spiritual development. Para Bhakti is not the effect of any action or effect or Sadhana done by the aspirant. If it is an effect, then it cannot be eternal.

Devotion is higher than the others, because it is its own reward. It is devotion for devotion's sake. It is love for love's sake. Therefore, Narada says Phalarupatvat. That is the reason why it excels others. Those who follow other paths cherish some ulterior motives in view. So they fail to attain God.

ईश्वरस्याप्यभिमानद्वेषित्वाद् दैन्यप्रियत्वाच्च ॥२७॥

Sutra. 27. Easvarasyapyabhimanadveshitvad dainya priyattvaccha.

*(Devotion is higher than the others), because God hates egoism and loves humility.*

ईश्वरस्य Easvarasya: God's; अपि api: also; अभिमानद्वेषित्वाद् Abhimanadveshitvat; dislike or aversion for conceit or egoism; दैन्य प्रियत्वात् Dainyapriyatvat: love of meekness; च cha: and.

A Devotee absolutely depends upon God alone. He is in communion with the Lord. He is ever peaceful and blissful. Others run after powers, etc. They depend upon their self-effort. They fall and become miserable.

You should not think that God Himself is partial and subject to feeling of love and hatred. It simply means that egoism is a great obstacle to the realisation of God-consciousness. The more you empty your egoism the more your heart will be filled with God. The grace of God is always there. Only the ego prevents man from taking advantage of it.

For those who are proud of their wealth or position or learning or birth, spiritual discipline cannot come and they cannot realise God. They are myopic or short-sighted. Wealth is more a barrier than an aid to spirituality.

Those who tread the path of Jnana and Yoga are liable to become proud of their powers and wisdom. Bhaktas are humble. Humility is the foundation of Bhakti Yoga.

God has no hatred or partiality for anyone. All are equal in His eyes. His heart is full of love even for the proud. He delivers the proud and the haughty through punishment and the humble devotees, through affectionate caresses.

The Lord does not allow pride to grow in His devotees. Pride is the root of all sorrows. It is the cause of worldly bondage. It brings sufferings of various kinds.

Bhakti is absolute self-surrender. In true devotion there is no room for the pride of one's own efforts or spiritual discipline. A devotee feels that he is an instrument in the hands of God and God does everything for him. There is not the slightest trace of ego. Therefore, the path of devotion is superior to all other paths.

In the practice of Jnana Yoga the aspirant has to depend upon himself alone. For a Bhakta the grace of God descends. God is Bhakta Vatsala, Dinanatha, Dinabandhu.

God dispenses according to the merit and demerit of the individual soul. So He is not partial and cruel.

It is not the fault of the fire if it warns a man who comes near it, but not one who is away from it.

This is another reason. Humility is the greatest of all virtues. All other virtues cling to the man who is endowed with humility. Gouranga Mahaprabhu was an embodiment of meekness. He sat in the place where shoes were kept, when he wanted to have an interview with a learned Pundit. Pride is a thorn in Bhakti Marga. It destroys devotion and all other virtues. Pride is ignorance. One can win the hearts of all by humility. A Bhakta should be humbler than the blade of grass which is trodden by the feet. That man only can sing always Hari's name. It is difficult to develop this virtue. One has to kill himself and remain like a block of stone. The stiff egoism asserts again and again.

In the Bible you will find: "Blessed are the poor in spirit, for theirs is the kingdom of heaven. Blessed are the meek, for they shall inherit the earth." Lord Jesus speaks very highly of this virtue, humility, in his sermon on the mount.

Just as fire removes the sensation of cold only of those who approach it, so also God removes the bondage of those who worship Him with earnestness and approach Him through daily prayer, right conduct and meditation.

Krishna said to Radha: "There are those who think themselves separate from Me. I rob them of their all and then when they see Me, all the ties of the world disappears. There are those, the worldly-minded, who kill the Self in them. I am cruel to them, but even to them I am kind for I confer happiness upon them in their grief. All souls are my favourites; I play many games with them till they forget all that is selfish, till they love Me for the sake of love alone, as thou now doest, O Radha!"

# KNOWLEDGE AND DEVOTION

## तस्य ज्ञानमेव साधनमित्येके ॥२८॥

**Sutra 28. Tasya jnanameva sadhanamityeke.**

*In the view of some, knowledge (of the object loved) alone is the means to attain (devotion).*

तस्य Tasyah: of that supreme Love; ज्ञानम् Jnanam: Knowledge; एव eva: alone; साधनम् Sadhanam: means; इति iti: thus एके eke: some (teachers think).

Bhakti must be preceded by the knowledge that the object of one's devotion and worship is the Lord, who is Omnipotent, Omniscient, All-Merciful, who possesses infinite auspicious qualities, who is the support and substratum of all, etc. Without this knowledge, there will be no faith in God, without faith there will be no attachment to God, and without attachment there will be no lasting and intense devotion.

Jnana here is not Brahma Jnana. It is only an ordinary understanding.

Some say: Even in the worldly parlance, knowledge comes first. Through knowledge of a thing, one gets love for that object. A girl gets knowledge of her would-be husband: He can sing well, He is beautiful. He has passed his I.C.S. Examination. He is now a district magistrate...and so on. A patient gets knowledge of the virtuous qualities of barley. Then he loves barley and takes with delight bread made of barley. He knows it is cooling and sattvic and so on. So also one gets knowledge of God at first. Then he begins to love. Therefore, "Jnanam" is the 'Sadhanam" or means for devotion.

Devotion to God may be developed through mere faith and reverence. Jatayu, Gajendra, Dhruva, Sabari realised God through mere devotion. In the love of the child to the mother, there is no understanding. So the view that Jnana is the Sadhana of devotin is only partially true.

अन्योन्याश्रयत्वमित्यन्ये ॥२९॥

**Sutra 29. Anyonyasrayatvamityanye.**

*Others are of opinion that there is mutual dependence between knowledge and devotion.*

अन्योन्याश्रयत्वम् Anyonya-asreyatvam: Mutual dependence (of knowledge and devotion); इति iti; thus, so अन्ये anye: others

Here knowledge does not mean God-vision.

One cannot know God without love and without exertion. It is not possible to love truly without knowing the object of his love and without exerting to serve his beloved. It is not also possible to exert oneself for someone without knowing and loving him. All the faculties of the mind always co-operate with one another.

"Anyonya-asraya" is mutual dependence. The wife is depending upon the husband for her wants, clothing, food and attendance while she is sick. The husband is depending upon his wife for his food and other kinds of service. This is mutual dependence. The king depends upon the subjects for his revenue. The subjects depend upon the king for their protection, water supply, sanitation, lighting and medical aid. This is also a case of mutual dependence.

Even so devotion depends upon knowledge and knowledge upon devotion.

In the Gita you find: *"Sradhavan labhyate jnanam*-the man who is full of faith obtained wisdom." Ch. IV-39.

*"Tesham satata yuktanam bhajatam pritipurvakam, Dadami buddhi yogam tam yena mamupayantite."*

"To these, ever harmonious (worshipping in love) I give the Yoga of discrimination by which they come unto Me." Ch. X-10.

"By devotion he knoweth Me in essence, who and what I am; having thus known Me in essence he forthwith entereth into the Supreme." — Ch. XVIII-55.

## स्वयं फलरूपतेति ब्रह्मकुमारः ॥३०॥

**Sutra 30. Svayam phalarupateti brahmakumarah.**

*Bhakti is its own fruit — thus opines Brahmakumara (Narada), the son of Brahma.*

स्वयम् Svayam: of itself; फलरूपता Phalarupata (Bhakti): being its won fruit; इति Iti: thus; so; ब्रह्मकुमारः Brhamakumarah: Son of Brhama i.e., Narada (Manyate: thinks).

Narada holds that devotion is both the end and the means.

Bhakti is both the root and fruit of the tree of spirituality.

Bhakti is self-sufficent. It does not depend on any other Sadhana.

There is nothing superior to Bhakti for the realisation of which it may be used as a means. A true devotee practises devotion for its own sake. According to Bhakti Yoga, school, knowledge and wisdom are subordinate to devotion.

From what has devotion resulted? From devotion itself. Bhakti is both the cause and the effect.

Bhakti is not the fruit or result of any practice. All practices enjoined by the scriptures are only to remove the ego or the veil.

Bhakti has no cause. It is not the effect or anything else also.

### राजगृहभोजनादिषु तथैव दृष्टत्वात् ॥३१॥

**Sutra 31. Rajagrihabhojanadishu tathaiva drishtatvat.**

*For it is seen to be just so in the case of the king, home and dinner.*

राजगृहभोजनादिषु Raja-griha-bhojana-dishu: in the case of the king, home and dinner; तथा tatha: in similar manner; एव eva: only; दृष्टत्वात् drishtavat; because it has been seen.

Narada gives here three illustrations to explain his view that the experience of bliss by a Bhakta in the presence of the Lord is not the result of any prctice.

Once a king lost his son in a forest. The prince was found by a forester. He grew in the forest under the care of the forester. Neither the forester nor the child knew that the child was a prince. Later on the truth was known and the prince has taken to his kingdom.

Druing the period that the prince stayed with the forester, he had not been any other than the prince. After he came into his kingdom also, he was not any other than the prince.

When the boy, who was ignorant of his parentage, and who considered himself a mere forester, heard of his parentage accidentally, nothing new is produced but he is only reminded of an existing fact. Even so, one is reminded of one's true status when one realises the supreme Self.

Just as the boy had been the prince all along, a devotee has devotion in him before the time when he begins his spiritual practices, during the period of his practices and even afterwards.

A man goes on a long pilgrimage. For many days he wanders about and endures many hardships. He experiences severe kinds of troubles. He cannot enjoy, during his journey, the conveniences which he enjoyed in his own home. The home continues to be his home even in his absence but the distance which stood in the way of his enjoyment is removed when he comes back. The pleasurable experiences are again revived as soon as he comes back. Nothing new is produced by his coming back.

If the devotee goes away from the presence of the Lord as the pilgrim goes away from his own home, he denies himself the happiness for the time being. But if he practises devotion to the Lord he will reach his own home and commune with the Lord and enjoy the divine bliss.

When a man is hungry, he is unhappy. The food does not produce any new satisfaction but only removes the disturbance caused by hunger. It removes hunger, the source of unhappiness. When the uneasiness is removed, the natural satisfaction remains undisturbed.

These illustrations indicate how spiritual practices really work. Then remove only the obstructions to the natural experience of the Self, which is external and never produced by any effort on the part of man.

## न तेन राजपरितोष क्षुधाशान्तिर्वा ॥३२॥

**Sutra 32. Na tena rajaparitosha kshudhasantirva.**

*Not by that (by mere knowledge of things) does the king become king, nor does the hungry man become satisfied.*

न Na: not; तेन tena: by that; राज Raja; king: परितोष Paritosha: satisfaction: क्षुधाशान्तिः Kshudhasanti: appeasement of hunger; वा va: or.

Not as a result of the hearing of the news does the boy become a prince. He was a prince already. No status was added to him by his mere hearing.

The pilgrim's satisfaction is also there already. Nothing new was added to him by his return to his home.

Mere knowledge of the food and its ingredients cannot satisfy your hunger. You must eat the food. Then alone satisfaction will come and hunger will be appeased. Even so mere verbal knowledge of God cannot develop devotion and give peace.

The illustrations are intended to warn students against supposing that mere intellectual knowledge of God is quite sufficient.

The followers of the path of devotion oppose those who hold the view that knowledge is means for attainment of devotion by the aid of the above illustration. They say: "Mere knowledge of food cannot appease hunger; so also mere knowledge cannot develop devotion."

## तस्मात्सैव ग्राह्या मुमुक्षुभिः ॥३३॥

**Sutra 33. Tasmatsaiva grahya mumukshubhihi.**

*Therefore the path of devotion alone should be adapted by those who desire salvation.*

तस्मात् Tasmat: therefore; hence; (since devotion is

higher than the other paths); सा Sa: supreme devotion, that; एव Eva, alone (to the exclusion of the others); मुमुक्षुभिः Mumukshubhihi: by seekers of liberation; ग्राह्या Grahya: worthy of being adapted (as the goal).

In the foregoing 32 Sutras the nature of Para Bhakti has been described and explained.

The royal road to liberation is devotion to God. Devotion is a sure, natural and easy means to liberation.

There are few people who are really intellectual enough to grasp the subtleties of the metaphysics of Sri Sankara. The path of devotion alone is possible for the vast majority of us.

The path of devotion ends at the same path as the path of Knowledge Para Bhakti or Jnana are one.

Devotion cuts asunder the worldly bondage easily. It attracts God Himself who becomes the object of our love and adoration.

Final emancipation is very difficult to attain but that very salvation forces itself upon the devotee unsolicited.

Therefore aspirants should practise devotion and devotion alone.

You must become a *Mumukshu*. You should pine for liberation. You should not desire anything other than the Lord. Then alone God will choose you. Then alone the Lord stretches out His hand to lift you up from the mire of this Samsara.

Attachment assumes various subtle forms even in aspirants. It lingers even in the mind of the great in the name of patriotism, institution, organisation, religion, service for humanity, etc. You must cut all sorts of attachment ruthlessly. Then alone you will develop *Ananya Bhakti*.

'Sadhana' means discipline.

Para Bhakti Paramaprema or supreme love is the highest Realisation which is the nature of Moksha. For a devotee this is the summit of all values.

With the 33rd Sutra, the part dealing with Para Bhakti comes to an end. All the remaining Sutras of the book deal with the means for attaining Para Bhakti and God-Realisation.

In the next chapter, consisting of Sutra 34 to 50, the Sadhanas are mentioned.

# HOW TO DEVELOP BHAKTI

## तस्या साधनानि गायन्ति आचार्याः ॥३४॥

**Sutra 34. Tasya sadhanani gayanti acharyaha.**

*The teachers have sung (as follows) about the means (for the culture) of devotion.*

तस्या Tasya: its of that supreme love; साधनानि Sadhanani: means; गायन्ति Gayanti: sings; आचार्याः Acharyaha: Teachers.

The means here described are only accessory, because Bhakti is its own means as has been shown already.

'Acharya' does not merely mean teachers. It means those who are practising what they preach. "Chara" is to move. They move along the path about which they speak. They live the life of the highest Bhaktas of the Lord. They alone are really fit to teach. Their teaching alone will be the most effective. Acharyas or teachers are those who have had first hand experience of the discipline and the consequent Realisation.

*Apara Bhakti* (lower Bhakti) is the direct means to obtain *Para Bhakti* or supreme devotion which is Realisation itself.

Renunciation, detachment for worldly objects and practice (Abhyasa) form the corner stone of all spiritual discipline.

## तत्तु विषयत्यागात् संगत्यागाच्च ॥३५॥

**Sutra 35. Tattu Vishaya Tyagat Sangatyagaccha.**

*Devotion to God is attained by abandoning all sensual pleasures and all attachment to sensual objects.*

तत् Tat: that; (Prema, supreme devotion); तु Tu: now; विषयत्यागात् Vishayatyagat: from abandonment of sensual objects संगत्यांगात् Sangatyagat: from renunciation of attachment च cha: and.

The consciousness of 'I' and 'mine' in everything you do and deal with is the strongest of all attachments.

Sensual pleasures cause distraction of the mind. Sensual enjoyment weakens the will and renders the mind unfit for concentration and divine contemplation; generates cravings, destroys discrimination, dispassion, devotion and the power of enquiry into the nature of ultimate Truth.

If there is craving when objects are renounced, the renunciation is not true renunciation. Renounce the craving. This is real renunciation. There can be devotion in a mind only when the mind is freed from all cravings. One enjoys supreme bliss and peace through renunciation of objects of enjoyment.

There are five *Vishayas* corresponding to the five sense organs. They are *sabda* (sound), *sparsa* (touch), *rupa* (form), *rasa* (taste) and *gandha* (smell).

In *Vishaya Tyaga* you must destroy your liking for the objects by finding the *doshas* or defects in the objects. Objects are unreal. Objects are perishable. Pain is mixed with pleasure. If you keep the defects before your mind's eye, the mind will not run towards objects.

Do not allow the mind to dwell on memories of

pleasant objects. Do not allow the mind to think of objects. This is *Sanga Tyaga* or renunciation of association of objects.

Without *Tyaga* or renunciation no spiritual progress is possible.

One should practise internal and external renunciation. External renunciation is absolutely necessary in the early stages; while internal renunciation is essential at all times.

Renunciation of egoism is the best kind of renunciation. Renunciation is not complete until ego is totally annihilated.

In Kaivalya Upanishad you will find *"Na Karmana na prajaya dhanena, tyageneike amritatvamanasuh*— neither by actions nor by progeny nor by riches but by renunciation alone is immortality attained."

Here are the nine means of cultivating Bhakti. Sri Rama says to Sabari: "Herein, the culture of devotion is the first means, it has been taught, the company of the good; the second, conversation about My achievements; the third, recital of My virtues; the fourth, occupation of expounding My words; the fifth, O gentle one, constant and sincere worship of the preceptor, thinking that I am he; the sixth has been said to be virtuousness, self-restraint, observance, etc., and ever living attachment to My worship; the seventh is said to be religious service with every detail, reciting the Mantra specially applicable to Me; greater adoration to My votaries, consciousness of Me in all beings, indifference to external objects, together with internal peace, make up the eighth; and, O lady, the ninth is the consideration of My essence. O auspicious one, devotion in the form of love is produced in any and every one who  employs this means in the shape of ninefold (secondary or instrumental) devotion, no matter whether one is woman or a man or an inferior creation. And as soon as devotional love is produced, one feels My essence, as it were, and one who becomes accomplished by the awareness of Me, attains Me. He attains liberation even in this birth. Therefore, it is sure that devotion is the source of Salvation."

"Mindful of Me, their life hidden in Me, illumining, each other, even conversing about Me, they are content and joyful" Chap. X-9.

"Merge thy mind in Me, by My devotee, sacrifice to Me, prostrate thyself before Me, thou shalt come even to Me. I pledge thee My truth; thou art dear to Me." Chap. XVIII-65.

"United to the Reason, purified, controlling the self by firmness, having abandoned sound and the other objects of the senses, having laid aside passion and malice.

"Dwelling in solitude; abstemious; speech, body and mind subdued, constantly fixed in meditation and Yoga; taking refuge in dispassion.

"Having cast aside egoism, violence, arrogance, desire, wrath, covetousness, selfless and peaceful, he is fit to become the Eternal.

"Becoming Brahman, serene in the Self, he neither grieveth nor desireth, the same to all beings, he obtaineth supreme devotion unto Me." Chap. XVIII 51, 52, 53, 54.

## अव्यावृत भजनात् ॥३६॥

**Sutra 36. Avyavrita Bhajanat.**

*By uninterrupted worship (success is attained in the practice of devotion).*

अव्यावृत भजनात् Avyavrita-bhajanat: by uninterrupted worship.

This Sutra explains the foregoing one. In the previous Sutra it is said that devotion to God may be developed by abandoning objects of desire and attachment to objects. But how can one overcome this attraction? This answer is given in this Sutra.

The attraction or temptation of worldly desires may be overcome by uninterrupted worship of God.

There are many trials on the path of devotion viz., diseases, losses, frustrations, etc. The devotee should bear all these with great patience.

Lord Krishna says in the Gita, "O Arjuna! he who constantly thinks of Me, without any other thought, I am easily reached by that Yogi, who is thus ceaselessly attached to Me." VIII-14.

Maharshi Patanjali says in his aphorism on Raja Yoga, "Practice becomes rooted when it is ceaselessly carried on with reverence and zeal for a long time." 1.14.

You can make a rope out of sand, you can press oil out of sand, you can churn out butter from water but no one can cross over this formidable Samsara or ocean of births and deaths without ceaseless Bhajan or worship of the Lord.

Pooja, Seva are also Bhajan or worship. All kinds of service to the Lord in a spirit of devotion is Bhajan. Service to humanity with Divine Bhava is also worship or Bhajan.

To hear of Vishnu or the Lord, to sing His names and glories, to remember Him, to do His service, to worship Him with flowers, etc., to resign to Him all the works done, to offer the body to His service and care — all these are to be included in Bhajan.

Even sleeping, eating, etc., should be regarded as an

act of service or worship to the Lord . . . . . *Yadyat Karma Karomi Tat Tadakhilam sambo tavaradhanam.* Feel that it is the Lord within you who eats, sleeps, etc. The ego will be completely effaced. That is absolute surrender to the Lord."

In Sutra 35 the spiritual practice is of a negative character. It is avoidance of evil. But in this Sutra it is an active spiritual practice.

You must be a spiritual hero, an *Adhyatmic*, undaunted soldier. You must not be afraid of obstacles and difficulties. You must surmount them patiently and cross all the hurdles that stand in your spiritual path. Let the inner spiritual fire and aspiration burn steadily. Plod.on. Persevere, and come out victorious.

Yield not to weakness and temptations. Be vigilant. Be on the alert. Kill wanton negligence, sloth and carelessness.

Take rest. But rest is only a change of work. Do Kirtan. This will give you the needed rest. This will remove fatigue. Have reverence for the ideal. Create interest in the spiritual practices. Have variety such as *Mantra* writing, *Japa, Kirtan*, prayer, meditation, study, service, etc. All these are Bhajan or worship.

Worship by fits and starts will not do. It must be constant. It must be *Tailadharavat* (like flow of oil). If there is break, desires will try to enter the mind. Unholy thoughts and worldly temptations will ransack the Antahkarana. Rajas and Tamas will try to overcome you. There will·be resurrection of old desires. The devotee will have to be very vigilant and cautious. That is the reason why Lord Krishna says: *"sarveshu kaleshu mam anusmara* — At all times think of Me." Ch.VIII-7.

## लोकेऽपि भगवत् गुणश्रवणकीर्तनात् ।।३७।।

**Sutra 37. Lokepi Bhagavat guna Sravana kirtanat.**

*(Bhakti develops) from listening to and singing of the attributes and glories of the Lord, even while engaged in the ordinary activities of life in the world.*

लोके Loke: in society; while engaged in the ordinary activities of life in the world; अपि api: also, even; भगवत् गुण श्रवण कीर्तनात् Bhagavadguna-Sravana-kirtanat: from listening to and singing of the attributes and glories of the Lord.

The Lord says, "I do not dwell in Vaikuntha (the abode of Vishnu, the highest heaven), nor in the hearts of Yogins, O Narada, I dwell there where my devotees sing."

In this world instances are found which indicate that devotion to God may be cultivated by listening to and singing of the attributes of God.

Divine life and ordinary life should not be separated. All activities may be turned into worship if only you do not forget the constant remembrance of the Lord and if you keep up the divine *bhava* or right mental attitude during work.

The ears that do not hear the glories of the Lord are like holes in the earth where snakes dwell. The tongue that does not sing the praises of God is as useless as the tongue of a pig.

The Name uttered knowingly or unknowingly burns up sins just as fire burns fuel.

He who does the *Kirtan* and *Japa* of Lord's names derives the merit of all austerities, of all sacrifices, of baths in all sacred waters, and of study of the Vedas.

Just as the sun removes the darkness of mountain

caves, just as the powerful wind makes a heavy cloud to vanish, even so, the *Kirtan* and *Japa* of the divine name enter the heart and bring all sorrows and miseries to an end.

Therefore, the constant practice of *Kirtan*, hearing and remembrance of the name and glory of God is surely the best and supreme method for the attainment of devotion and God-realisation.

Bhagavata says, "To a man tossed and distressed in the wild fire of *Samsara,* there is no boat other than constant listening to and drinking of the excellent essence of the Leelas and glories of the Lord to cross this ocean of *Samsara.*" —4-40.

*Japa* and *Kirtan* form the highest help to meditation, self-purification and realisation. The aspirant reaches the highest by *Japa and Kirtan. Japa* is the most excellent sacrifice. It gives the best result. He who does *Japa* gets the fruit of all sacrifices.

*Japa* and *Kirtan* can be practised by all irrespective of age, sex, caste, and stages of life, at all times and in all places.

Restraint of mind, purity, silence, freedom from distraction constitute the success in *Japa.*

Japa must be accompanied by meditation on the meaning of the *Mantra.* Then one will attain God-realisation quickly.

Sounds of *Mantras* generate special kind of vibrations in the body, mind and the atmosphere which are highly beneficial for spiritual practice.

Om Namah Sivaya, Om Namo Narayanaya, Om Namo Bhagavate Vasudevaya, Om Sri Ram Jaya Ram Jaya Jaya Ram are Siddha Mantras. Siddha Mantras are special

Mantras which have been tested and found to be effective in actual use in the past. Those who recite these Siddha Mantras attain God-realisation quickly.

Bhagavan is free from all imperfections. He is perfect. Wisdom, dispassion, power, glory, dominion and splendour are the six attributes of God. Bhaga indicates the six attributes of God. Meditation on Bhagavan will lead to the attainment of Bhagavan.

*"Kalau Kesava Kirtanat"* — in the Kali Yuga, salvation is attained by Kirtan or singing the praises of God." People have not got good physique and unbroken Brahmacharya to practise Hatha Yogic Kriyas such as *Pranayama, kumbhaka, Khechari mudra*, etc. They lack in bold understanding, gigantic intellect and strong will to understand and practise Vedanta. The easy way is Kirtan only.

मुख्यतस्तु महत्कृपयैव भगवत्कृपालेशाद्वा ॥३८॥

**Sutra 38. Mukhyatastu mahatkripayaiva bhagavatkripaleshadva.**

*But it (devotion) is obtained chiefly by the grace of great men or through a slight measure of Divine grace.*

मुख्यतः Mukhyatah: chiefly; तु tu:but; महत्कृपया Mahatkripaya: by the grace of great men; एव Eva: only; भगवत्कृपालेशात् Bhagavat-kripa-lesat: through a slight measure of the grace of the Lord; वा Va: or.

In the preceding three Sutras the devotees' exertion was emphasised, e.g. *Vishaya tyagat sangatyagat cha"*: abandoning of objects and attachment; *"Avyavrita Bhajanat,"* ceaseless worship and *"Bhagavat-Guna-Sravana-Kirtanat"* hearing of the glories of the Lord and Kirtan or singing the names and glories of the Lord.

In this Sutra and the next three, the descent of the Lord's grace is referred to.

When the great men are moved by compassion towards their mortal brothers, the Lord works through them.

In Srimad Bhagavata it is said, "In the company of great prevail talks which perfectly convey My majesty and which soothe the heart and the ear. From listening to these, faith, attachment and devotion will succeed one another towards Him who is the way to salvation."

Self-effort is certainly necessary. The aspirant will soon realise that he can do nothing by himself and that he can attain God-realisation only through the grace of the great ones, through even a little grace of the Lord.

Even a moment's contact or *Satsanga* with saints and sages is highly beneficial. *Satsanga* destroys all worldly attachments and desires and cravings.

Bhakti cannot be cultivated without association with saints.

Divine grace can be obtained through the grace of Mahatmas or great souls.

Self-effort is possible only through Divine grace. Divine grace comes automatically as a result of good actions, devotion and self-surrender. When the ego is annihilated or effaced, the obstruction to the flow of divine grace is removed and the divine grace freely flows.

The Guru will appear only through the grace of the Lord. He transmutes his power to the disciple through look, touch or *Sankalpa*. The Lord alone appears as a Guru. The Guru acts under the guidance of the Lord.

The Vedantins are in favour of self-effort, while the followers of the path of devotion always advocate the doctrine of divine grace. The devotees say that self-effort is also necessary for self-purification and for enabling grace to manifest itself. An extreme school of Bhakti says that even self-effort is made possible only by the Lord's grace.

Why all men are not saved by the Lord's grace? The Lord has given through His grace free will to everyone to choose between good and evil. He must, therefore, wait till he of his own accord turns to the Lord. As man is endowed with a free will, God will wait to see man's predeliction for Him.

The doctrine of free will and the doctrine of grace can be satisfactorily reconciled. Some explain that the law of Karma is an aspect of grace, as the Lord would otherwise be interfering with the individual's freedom. The Lord does not want to free the individual soul to do anything against its own likes and dislikes.

Others say that grace is only aspect of Karma. Good acts such as devotion and self-surrender produce their result, namely, grace of God under the law of Karma.

Lord Krishna says; "This divine illusion of Mine, caused by the qualities, is hard to pierce; they who come to Me, they cross over this illusion." Gita Ch.VII-14. In Mundaka Upanishad and Kathopanishad you will find, "This Atman cannot be attained by discourse, nor by intelligence nor by profound study. It can be realised by him only whom it favours; him this Atman favours with its manifestation." "Bhagavat Kripa lesat- —" Even a drop of grace is quite sufficient to free oneself from the trammels of this Samsara. It is through the grace of the Lord alone that a man can stick to the spiritual path and break all sorts of ties and attachments.

"Though ever performing all actions, taking refuge in Me, by My grace he obtains the eternal indestructible abode." Gita Ch. XVIII-56.

"Thinking on Me, thou shalt overcome all obstacles by My grace; but if from egoism thou wilt not listen thou shalt be destroyed utterly." Gita Ch. XVIII-58.

"Out of pure compassion for them, dwelling within their Self, I destroy the ignorance-born darkness by the shining lamp of wisdom. "Gita Ch. X-II.

"*Mahat-Kripa*" – the grace of the great ones is also necessary. There is no difference between God and a realised Bhagavata. Both are identical. There is no hope of overhauling the old vicious Samskaras of a worldly man without the help of *Satsanga* of Mahatmas. *Satsanga* is a safe boat to take the aspirant to the other shore of fear-lessness, the shore which is beyond darkness. The glory of *Satsanga* is vividly eulogised in the Bhagavata, the Ramayana and all scriptures. Books written by realised persons constitute secondary Satsanga. When you study them you are in holy communion with the authors.

Grace will descend only on those aspirants who are earnestly struggling in the path and are thirsting for realisation. Nowadays people want to lead a life of ease and expect the grace of Mahatmas. They themselves do not want to do any kind of *Tapas* or Sadhana. They want a magic pill to put them in *Samadhi* at once. They want worldly comforts and realisation in one and the same cup.

Kabir, Tulasidas, Sankara and Guru Nanak have all written volumes on the glory of Satsanga with Mahatmas. Faith in God, in scriptures, attachment and devotion to God, slowly develop in those who are regular in Satsanga.

There is complaint by householders nowadays that there are no good Mahatmas. This is a lame excuse. The company of Sadhus is a question of supply and demand. If there is a sincere demand the supply will come at once. This is the inexorable law of nature. If you are really thirsty you will find your Master at your very threshold. You lead a happy-go-lucky life, your mind is full of passion and unholy Vasanas. You do not care a bit for higher, divine life. You waste your time in idle gossiping and vain worldly talks. You have become a hopeless slave of passion, greed and name and fame. And yet you complain: "I cannot get Satsanga". Blame yourself first. Admit your faults. Repent sincerely for your mistakes. Do *Prayaschitta*. Fast. Pray. Cry bitterly in solitude. Make yourself a deserving *Adhikari* first. Then come to me. I shall put you in the right path, guide you and elevate you to sublime heights. These 'oversouls' or high souls are waiting to get hold of the right type of aspirants. Mahatmas are in plenty. Real seekers are few. If you bring a charge: "There are no good Mahatmas," Mahatmas also will bring a serious charge: "There are no real seekers after Truth."

# GLORY OF THE COMPANY OF THE WISE

## महत्सङ्गस्तु दुर्लभोऽगम्योऽमोघश्च ॥३९॥

**Sutra 39. Mahatsangastu durlabho agamya amoghascha.**

*The company of the great souls is again difficult of attainment, is unapproachable and is infallible or unfailing in its effect.*

महत्संगः Mahatsangah: company of the great; तु tu: again; but, then; दुर्लभः Durlabhah: difficult to obtain; अगम्य Agamya: unapproachable; subtle and incomprehensible, inscrutable; अमोघः Amogha: unerringly effective; च cha: and.

Lord Krishna says in the Gita, "One in a thousand struggle for Self-realisation and even among such aspirants only one in a thousand attains Self-realisation."

Be not duped by a false spiritual guide.

You may not be able to recognise a really worthy spiritual preceptor even after coming into contact with him, because great souls generally hide their greatness. An aspirant who has earned great merits by his strenuous endeavour in the present life or previous ones will be able to recognise the greatness of a Mahatma and obtain his grace. The lazy and indolent have no chance of obtaining the grace of a great soul.

You should not accept any one and everyone as Guru. Teachers of real spiritual enlightenment are very rare.

To be a Guru one must have command from God.

The effect of saintly contact is unerring or infallible. In ordinary aspirants the transformation may be slow and gradual.

The spiritual waves set up by a saint travel a very long distance, reach the proper *adhikari* and transform them.

Good things are always rare in this world. Musk, saffron, radium, sandalwood, learned persons, virtuous persons, heroes, philanthrophists, etc., are rare. When such is the case, what to speak of saints, Yogins, Jnanins, and Bhaktas! You will have to equip yourself first with the necessary qualifications of self-restraint, celibacy, calmness of mind, keen desire for liberation, humility, obedience, spirit of service, etc., to make yourself fit for their company. If you get their company the question of your salvation is solved. Sri Sankara says in his Vivekachudamani, "Three things are rare in this world. They are 1. human birth, 2. Desire for liberation and 3. the care of a perfected sage."

## लभ्यतेऽपितत्कृपयैव ॥४० ॥

### Sutra 40. Labhyateapi tat kripayaiva.

*The company of the Great Ones is obtained by the grace of God alone.*

लभ्यते Labhyate: is obtained; अपि Api: nevertheless, and; तत्कृपया tat-kripaya: by His (God's grace); एव Eva: only.

In the previous Sutra, it was stated that the company of the great is *"Durlabha"* difficult, *"Agamya"* unapproachable, but *"Amogha"* infallible or unfailing in its effects. One is apt to be discouraged by such a statement. In this Sutra encouragement is given. It says *"api"* even though it is difficult, etc., yet Labhyate'—it is obtained.

The company of the Guru or great one is obtained. It is an act of divine grace. *"Tat kripaya eva."*

When the time is ripe the Guru and disciple are brought together by the Lord in a mysterious way.

तस्मिन्स्तज्जने भेदाभावात् ॥४१॥

**Sutra 41. Tasminsthajjane bhedabhavat.**

*Because there is no difference between the Lord and His devotees.*

तस्मिन् Tasmin: in Him; तज्जने Tatjane: in His creatures; भेदाभावात् Bheda-abhavat: because of the absence of difference.

The devotee is God Himself. He who serves a devotee serves God Himself. The devotee dwells in the heart of God and God dwells in the heart of the devotee. In the Bhagavata the Lord says, "Devotees are My heart, and I am the heart of the devotees. They know nobody other than Me and I know nobody else than them."

The Gopis imitated the various sports of Lord Krishna. They entirely lost themselves, and knew not who they were.

When the individual soul surrenders himself to the Lord, he comes entirely under the influence and protection of the Lord. He is not affected by Maya. All differences are wiped out.

*"Tat-Jane".* It means people devoted to Tat i.e., devotees.

When the impurities in the mind are removed, the devotee recognises that there is no difference between him and the Lord. Then the divine grace descends. The grace may appear as the Guru. The grace may come in the form of concentration, serenity, devotion, vision of the Lord.

The Lord is not partial to anybody. His grace is available to all without any distinction. It is Lord's grace that drives a man to seek a Guru and to attain perfection.

God-realisation becomes natural and easy when a man willingly surrenders his whole being to the inflow of the divine grace. The ignorant man impedes the path of grace by his conceit, arrogance and egoism.

Just as a river loses its name and form after it has entered the ocean, so also a devotee loses his individuality when he merges himself in the Lord. The mind that causes distinction is annihilated by devotion.

## तदेव साध्यतां तदेव साध्यताम् ॥४२॥

### Sutra 42. Tadeva sadhyatam tadeva sadhyatam.

*Let that alone be practised, let that alone be practised.*

तत् Tat: that (aids to love of God referred to in Sutras 35-37); एव Eva: only alone; साध्यताम् Sadhyatam: let it be practised.

Tat: that, refers to renunciation and loving service described in Sutras 35-37 as well as the grace of God and Maha-purushas or great souls. Self-surrender must be complete. Then alone the divine grace will flow. Self-surrender is *Prapatti*.

Strive after love of God alone, strive after love of God alone.

Work for, strive after, the grace of God. Make serious efforts to obtain the grace of God. The object of repeating the phrase is to stress its urgency and importance.

Such practices as would enable us to obtain their grace alone should be adopted.

Therefore, cultivate this, cultivate this (contact with the lover of God, or Mahatma).

If you wish to cultivate divine love, sincerely long for the company of saints. Through the grace of the Lord you will obtain the company of great souls or Mahatmas, Mahapurushas.

Eva: that alone. That alone is valuable. Other things are of no value. God's grace alone must be obtained. The methods have already been given – detachment, service, kirtan, hearing of Lord's Leelas, etc.

# GIVE UP EVIL COMPANY

## दुस्संगः सर्वथैव त्याज्यः ॥४३॥

**Sutra 43. Dussangah sarvathaiva tyajyah.**

*Evil company should be certainly given up by all means.*

दुःसंगः Duh-sangah: evil company; सर्वथा Sarvatha: by all means; एव eva: only, certainly; त्याज्यः Tyajya: to be given up.

Everywhere, at all times, by all means avoid the company of the wicked.

A neophyte who keeps company with the wicked people or worldlings, loses his devotion and develops evil qualities. He also comes to the level of a worldly man. Mind imitates. Evil company is the main obstacle to devotion.

In the company of the wicked one develops immorality, licentiousness, vicious habits, voluptuousness, sensuality, hypocrisy, arrogance, etc. Evil company destroys all virtues such as purity, truthfulness, compassion, etc.

If the locality, food, surroundings, environment, vocation, form of worship, topics of discussion, books you read are Sattvic you will grow in spirituality and virtue. If they are Rajasic or Tamasic you will develop evil traits.

Some people argue "Why should we shun evil company? Is not God there also? Why should we see evil anywhere? Shall we not see only the good? Should we not see only God in the evil also?

A sage alone is above good and evil. He alone sees good in the evil too. For him there is neither good nor evil. He alone will not be affected by evil. He sees God in evil also. Ordinary man and a raw aspirant will be easily affected by evil company. He cannot see good in evil. Evil is a solid reality for him.

God is everywhere. God is in pure water, and in dirty water. But you cannot drink the dirty water. You cannot eat excreta. A young aspirant cannot take refuge in the Upanishadic saying, "All indeed is Brahman" when he is in the midst of temptations. Every object that stimulates lower passions must be ruthlessly avoided.

If the great saying, "All is Brahman" is taught to raw aspirant or half-baked neophyte or half-awakened student he will be ruined like Virochana who preached the philosophy of flesh to his disciples and followers.

This sublime instruction should only be imparted to the aspirant who is endowed with absolute moral purity, discrimination, dispassion and who is free from cravings for sensual pleasures.

Evil is a product of ignorance. Good is that which leads you to the attainment of God-realisation or eternal bliss. Evil is that which leads you to sorrow, unhappiness, misery, birth and death. Sattva is goodness. Tamas and Rajas are evils. Sattva will give serenity tranquillity, composure, calmness. Rajas and Tamas will cause agitation, restlessness, anxiety, vexation, suffering and unhappiness.

Bilvamangal once attended the nautch party of Chintamani. His whole *antahkarana* was poisoned. He was the virtuous son of a pious Brahmin. All his good traits disappeared. He fell in love with her. He ruined his life. There are thousands of such instances like this. In the Andhra province Vemana also was spoiled by evil company in the beginning.

Novels, cinemas, sight of pairing of animals, obscene scenery, vulgar music, nude pictures, anything that excites passion are all evil companies. There is nothing more dangerous than evil company. If the wife has no religious tendencies and is of worldly nature, her company also is tantamount to evil company. That is the reason why scriptures speak very highly of solitary places in Himalayas and on the banks of the Ganga.

कामक्रोधमोहस्मृतिभ्रंशबुद्धिनाशसर्वनाशकारणत्वात् ॥४४॥

### Sutra 44. Kamakrodhamoha smritibhramsa buddhinasa sarvanasakaranatvat.

*Because it is the cause of lust, anger, delusion, loss of memory, loss of intellect and total ruin.*

काम Kama: desire, lust; क्रोध Krodha: anger; मोह Moha: delusion, infatuation, bewilderment; स्मृतिभ्रंश smritibhramsa: loss of memory; बुद्धिनाश Buddhinasa: loss of intellect; सर्वनाश Sarvanasa: total ruin; कारणत्वात् Karanatvat: being the cause of.

Memory and intellect spoken of in this Sutra refer to meditation and pure reason or discrimination respectively.

Loss of memory is forgetfulness of the truth and forgetfulness of one's object in life as well as one's duty. *Buddhinasa* is death of discriminative reason.

Worldly minded people may talk of pleasurable worldly experiences and attractive objects seen by them. A novice in the spiritual path or even a spiritually advanced soul who has not attained Self-realisation, who is not rooted in the conviction of the utterly illusory nature of the world, will be impressed by such experiences. He may feel a desire to enjoy them.

Desire is born of Rajas. It generates both greed and anger. It is the cause for commission of sin.

The opposite of evil company "Dussanga" is "Satsanga".

The natural tendency of the mind is to stick to something. It is normally sticking to Vishaya or objects. If this tendency is to be annihilated, it must be turned to God or Atman.

"Buddhinasa" or loss of discrimination refers to the inability to distinguish between truth and falsehood, the permanent and the impermanent, good and bad, right and wrong, etc.

If the mind deviates even a little bit from its aim through lack of dispassion and vigilance, it will fall down and down like a ball dropped on the first step of the stairs. Therefore, be cautious, be vigilant.

Lord Krishna says: "Man thinking on the objects of sense, develops an attachment to these; from attachment arises desire; from desire anger proceeds; from anger arises delusion; from delusion confused memory; from confused memory the destruction of reason; from destruction of reason he perishes." Gita Ch. II-62-63. "It is desire, it is wrath, begotten by the quality of mobility, all-consuming, all-polluting, know thou this as our foe here on earth."

Ch. III-37. "Triple is the gateway to hell, destructive of self—lust, wrath, and greed, therefore, let man renounce these three." Ch. XVI-21. Tulasidasji says: "Wherever there is Kama there is no Rama" and wherever there is Rama there is no Kama.

तरङ्गायिता अपीमे संगात्समुद्रायन्ति ॥४५॥

**Sutra 45. Tarangayita apime sangatsamudrayanti.**

*Though they (evil tendencies, lust, anger, etc.) rise only in the form of ripples in the beginning, they become like an ocean as a result of evil company.*

तरङ्गयिता Tarangayitah: acting as ripples; अपि api: even though: इमे Ime: these (lust, anger, etc.); संगात् Sangat: by (evil) association; समुद्रायन्ति Samudrayanti: become like an ocean.

An aspirant should be afraid of even faint traces of evil till they are totally eradicated. Just as fire under the ashes may assume the form of a huge flame by the blowing of a strong wind, so also suppressed evil may assume a huge form through evil company.

Therefore, the aspirant should be ever vigilant and avoid evil company ruthlessly.

In the beginning lust and anger may be checked when they are in the form of ripples; but it is very difficult to curb them when they assume the form of a big ocean owing to evil company.

Drinking, meat-eating, hearing vulgar music, company of prostitutes, attendance of nautch party, theatres and cinemas excite passion and throw the victim into the hell of fire. Cinema has become a curse even in India. An officer spends half of his salary on cinema and runs into debts. All have developed a bad habit for some kind of sight-seeing. They cannot remain without it. The eyes want to see some kind of lights and sensational pictures. Cinema is a very good paying business nowadays. Various sorts of half-nude pictures and obscene sights are shown on the screen. College boys and young girls are unduly thrown into a state of mental excitement. Various sorts of evils are propagated. Cinema is an enemy of devotion. It is havocking the world. It should be entirely boycotted. It does immense harm to people. It is a great drain on the resources of man. It is a great temptation. All bad films should be thoroughly censored. Films should be passed by a religious body before they are brought on the screen. Only films which contain religious stories that are calculated to develop the moral and philosophical aspect of man may be allowed to come on the screen. A bill should be passed in the Parliament to this effect. This is a most important matter. All thoughtful men should direct their attention on this point.

It is gratifying to note that highly educated men and women of India take part in the cinema. College education alone will not do. If they want to impress people and to do real spiritual good to the world they should lead a life of Tapas and meditation and Brahmacharya.

# WHO CROSSES MAYA?

कस्तरति कस्तरति मायाम् ? यः सङ्गं त्यजति यो महानुभावं
सेवते निर्ममो भवति ॥४६॥

**Sutra 46. Kastarati kastarati mayam? Ya sangam tyajati yo mahanubhavam sevate, nirmamo bhavati.**

*Who crosses, who crosses the Maya? Only he who avoid all contact with such objects of senses as are likely to inflame passions, who resorts to a great spiritual soul and serves him and who is free from mineness or idea of possession.*

कः Kah: who; तरति tarati:crosses; कः kah: who; तरति tarati: crosses; मायाम् mayam: the world of senses; यः Yah: he who; संगं sangam: contact; त्यजति tyajati: gives up; यः Yah: who; महानुभावं Mahanubhavam: a great spiritual man; सेवते Sevate: resorts to and serves; निर्ममः Nirmamah: free from mineness; भवति Bhavati: becomes:

A Saint is the supreme refuge to those who are immersed in the formidable ocean of Samsara or worldly existence.

Worldly attachments and sins are easily got rid of through service to saints. Just as fire removes cold, fear and darkness, so also service to saints removes cold in the form of sin, fear of rebirth and the darkness of ignorance. Service to saints enables a man to develop devotion to God.

Maya is that illusory power of God which takes you away from reality and attracts you to the fleeting, sensual

pleasure. The working of Maya is very subtle. It is very difficult to detect her. The aspirant must be very, very
vigilant.

*Kastarati; kastarati:* The question is asked twice. That
shows the difficulty of getting rid of Maya. The phrase is
repeated to add conviction to the answer.

*Sangam:* It is attachment for external objects. The real
and strong attachment is the attachment to the ego. The
latter attachment must be cut asunder first.

Sri Sankara says: *"Satsangatve nissangatvam, nissan-
gatve nirmohatvam, nirmohatve nischalatatvam, nis-
chalatatve jivanmukti."* By keeping company with the
Mahatmas, one becomes dispassionate. He gets *Vairagya.*
He does not like the company of worldly men. Then he
develops the state of *"Nirmohatva".* He becomes free from
infatuation or delusion. Then his mind becomes steady and
one-pointed and rests on the *Svarupa* or Essence. Then he
attains liberation or freedom.

यो विविक्तस्थानं सेवते, यो लोगबन्धमुन्मूलयति निस्त्रैगुण्यो
भवति, योगक्षेमं त्यजति ॥४७॥

Sutra 47. Yo viviktasthanam, sevate, yo lokabandhamun-
mulayati nistraigunyo bhavati, yogakshemam tyajati.

*He who resorts to a solitary and holy place, he who roots
out worldly desires or bonds, transcends the three Gunas and
gives up all ideas of acquisition and preservation.*

यः Yah: who ; विविक्तस्थानम् viviktasthanam: a lonely
and holy place; सेवते sevate: resorts to; यः yah: who;
लोकबन्धं Likabandham: worldly desires or bonds; उन्मूलयति
Unmulayati: roots out; निस्त्रैगुण्य nisthraigunya: free from

the effects of the three Gunas; भवति bhavati: becomes योगक्षेमम् Yogakshemam: acquisition and preservation; त्यजति Tyajati: gives up.

One's own heart itself is the most secret or lonely and sacred place for meditation.

A solitary place is one where the din and noise of the talk of sensual desires and craving for sensual objects do not penetrate.

Mere retirement to a forest is of little spiritual value. He who has cravings and desires meets temptations even in a forest. Inner solitude is essential. It is an aid in rooting out the binding force of world attractions or temptations.

When one lives in solitude social ties automatically get slackened. If the aspirant does enquiry and compares this world of misery, pain, disease, death and sorrow with the sublime, glorious and wonderful life in God, these ties are completely broken asunder.

A solitary place is favourable for the practice of detachment, dispassion or *Vairagya*. The aspirant can do what ever he likes. He is not disturbed by other people. He is forced to give up comforts and some objects which he likes best, because he cannot get them in a solitary place.

Loneliness is not advisable for all. Many will become lazy and unclean if they live in seclusion. An aspirant can develop ethical virtues only if he remains in the world. World is the best teacher. Advanced Sadhakas alone can remain in seclusion. They alone will be benefited.

The poet who liked loneliness sang: "O solitude! Where are thy charms?" Lord Krishna lays great stress on this solitude — *"Vivikta sevi"* — Gita Chapter XVIII-52. *Viviktadesa sevitvam"* — Chapter XIII-10. Solitude has immense advantages. The mind gets one-pointedness by itself without any effort. In the world there are many distractions on all sides and a beginner finds it impossible to fix his mind on his *Lakshya*. One can reach a certain stage either in Yoga, Bhakti or Jnana in the world. For attaining advanced stages solitude is indispensably required. Raja Janaka and Eknath are examples of solitariness. Further, they were all Yoga-Bhrastas, born with a lot of spiritual Samskaras acquired through drastic Sadhana in their previous lives.

There is bondage only in the earth plane, astral plane and mental plane (heaven). There is no bondage in *Maharloka, Janoloka, Tapoloka* and *Satyaloka*.

Sattva is the enlightening quality; Rajas is the inflaming quality and Tamas is the enveloping or obscuring quality. Sattva is light, harmony; Rajas is passion, motion; and Tamas is inertia, darkness. These are the forces that bind the soul to the world.

**Lokabandham:** They are the binding forces of the world. They are Rajas and Tamas, desires, cravings, attachments, sensual pleasures.

The whole Sadhana or practice is transcendence of the three Gunas.

By discipline, worship, by cultivating virtues, study, kirtan, meditation, service of the preceptor and the grace of the Lord, the devotee or the Yogi transcends all the three Gunas.

The feeling of 'mine-ness' grows through constant association with sensual objects. It is very difficult to eradicate this feeling of 'mine-ness'.

**Yoga Kshema:** Yoga means applying one's needs and

Kshema means the preservation of what is already in our possession.

In the spiritual sense Yoga means union with God or God-realisation or the practice of Yoga Sadhana or discipline through which God is realised. Kshema means maintaining one's progress on the path of God-realisation. As a devotee entirely depends upon God, as he is ever united with the Lord, the Lord Himself looks after the Yoga and Kshema of the devotee.

Lord Krishna says in the Gita. "Those who are exclusively devoted to Me and worship Me in a disinterested way, fixing their thought on Me, I Myself bear the burden of their Yoga and Kshema, as they are ever united with Me." Chapter IX-22.

When the aspirant develops intense Bhakti, he will be able to give up Yoga and Kshema.

The ideas of this Sutra come in the Gita, Chapter II-45. "The Vedas deal with the three Gunas; be thou above these three qualities, O Arjuna! Beyond the pairs of opposites, ever steadfast in purity, careless of possession, full of the Self."

यः कर्मफलं त्यजति कर्माणि संन्यस्यति
ततो निर्द्वन्द्वो भवति ॥४८॥

**Sutra 48. Yah karmaphalam tyajati, karmani sannyasyati tato nirdvandvo bhavati.**

*He who renounces the fruits of his actions and who renounces all actions goes beyond the pairs of opposites (such as pleasure and pain, good and bad, heat and cold)*

यः Yah: who; कर्मफलं Karmaphalam: the fruits of actions; त्यजति gives up; कर्माणि Karmani: actions; संन्यस्यति

Sannyasyati: renounces; ततः tatah: then, thereby; निर्द्वन्द्वः Nirdvandvah: free from pairs of opposites (such as pleasure and pain, good and bad, heat and cold): भवति Bhavati: becomes.

Whatever the devotee does, he does it for the sake of the Lord. He does not expect any reward for his actions. Further, he has no attachment to either Karma or its fruits.

When the devotee feels that he is an instrument in the hands of God, he renounces doership and agency. When the devotee does total self-surrender, God destroys his ego and begins to act through his organs. Now the devotee is freed from the pair of opposites.

"All actions" means here selfish actions (*Kamya Karmas*). One should renounce selfish actions. Life is not possible without some kind of activity. Selfless activities must be continued.

When the devotee dedicates the fruits of all his actions and the actions themselves to the Lord he is freed from the effects of virtuous and vicious deeds. He is not affected in the least by pleasure and pain resulting from the pain or loss of the result of actions. Such a devotee is beyond the effects of the Gunas. He is ever immersed in the remembrance of God. Selfish actions have no attraction for him.

What you call world is not this wall or stone or tree. The world is a play kept up by these pairs of opposites which affect the mind through the two mental currents — *raga-Dvesha*, attraction and repulsion or likes and dislikes. He who conquers these pairs of opposites really conquers the whole world. Heat and cold affect the body; and pleasure and pain affect the mind. He who transcends the

*Dvandvas* always keeps a balanced mind. This is an important sign or *linga* of a Jivanmukta.

यो वेदानपि संन्यस्यति केवलमविच्छिन्नानुरागं लभते ॥४९॥

**Sutra 49. Yo vedanapi sannyasyati, kevalamavichchin-nanuragam labhate.**

*He who abandons even the Vedas, even the rites and ceremonies prescribed by the Vedas and obtains undivided and undiluted and uninterrupted flow of love towards God.*

यः Yah: who; वेदान् Vedan: the sacred books, the Vedas; अपि api: even संन्यस्यति Sannyasyati: renounces; केवलम् Kevalam: undivided; unalloyed; अविच्छिन्नानुरागं Avichchinanuragam: uninterrupted flow of love; लभते lab-hate: attains.

By 'Veda' it is meant here the ritualistic portion of the Vedas. The man of realisation does not stand in need of the rituals prescribed by the Vedas but they may be performed in earlier stages as a means for God-realisation.

**Kevalam:** Love for God is not diluted with desires of any other kind such as pleasures of earth and heaven. The love that arises at this stage is never satisfied till God is realised. This love is the *Mukhya Bhakti* that directly leads to *Para Bhakti.*

Renunciation of Vedas really means renunciation of desires.

When the devotee advances in his devotion he gets merged in the Lord. He is not capable of performing any Vedic rite or worldly action. The devotee has realised the ultimate aim of all Vedas. The devotee does not deliberately renounce the Vedas. The Vedas themselves withdraw their control over him as he has realised the goal of his life. He is now above the injunctions and interdiction imposed by the Vedas.

Continuous flow of love without any break even for a second is *Avichchinna-anurag*. Vedas can afford no interest for a man who has got this kind of incessant flow of Prema. That is the reason why the Gita says: "All true Vedas are as useful to an enlightened Brahmin, as is a tank in a place covered all over with water." Ch. II. 46.

### स तरति स तरति स लोकांस्तारयति ॥५०॥

**Sutra 50. Sa tarati, sa tarati sa lokamastarayati.**

*He (verily) crosses (Maya), he crosses (this ocean of Samsara, all limitations), he helps mankind to cross (also).*

सः Sah: he; तरति tarati: crosses (Maya, or ocean of Samsara): सः sah: he ; तरति tarati: he crosses; सः sah: he; लोकान् Lokan; all the world, mankind; तारयति Tarayati: helps to cross.

He overcomes all limitations. He goes beyond Maya and helps others also to go beyond the sea of sufferings or the ocean of Samsara. He becomes a true saviour of the world. He sanctifies the entire universe.

The question raised in the 46th aphorism as to who crosses Maya has been answered in the succeeding aphorisms.

A Saint of God-realisation can lift others to the divine status in an instant. A weak swimmer cannot help a drowning man. He who is immersed in worldliness cannot elevate others to the status of divinity. He cannot give a God-consciousness to others.

**Anuraga:** referred to in the previous aphorism is the highest rung in the ladder of devotion. It is the only means that will help the aspirant to cross Maya and overcome all limitations. It will enable him after realisation to help others also in reaching the goal and crossing this formidable Samsara.

The means of attaining devotion and the marks of those who have attained such devotion have been described in all the above aphorisms.

In the next chapter, Devarishi Narada proceeds to delineate the nature of divine love, attaining which devotees are easily able to reach the pinnacle of divine glory.

This world is compared to an ocean (Bhavasagar). *Trishnas* are the crocodiles. *Vasanas* ˙are the whales or sharks. *Indriyas* are the rivers. The three Gunas sre the waves. *Raga Dvesha* are the ripples. Ignorance is the substratum. Egoism is the essence. Lord Krishna says: "Those verily who, renouncing all actions in Me, and intent on Me, worship meditating on Me,   with whole-hearted Yoga, these I speedily lift up from the ocean of death and existence, O Partha; their minds being fixed on Me." Gita Ch. XII-6,7.

# NATURE OF PREM

## अनिर्वचनीयं प्रेमस्वरूपम् ॥५१॥

**Sutra 51. Anirvachaniyam premasvarupam.**

*The nature of love towards God is inexplicable in words.*

अनिर्वचनीयम् Anirvachaniyam: (is) incapable of being described precisely, not capable of being expressed words; प्रेमस्वरूपम् Premasvarupam: the nature of love.

The intrinsic nature of divine love defies precise definition or description. Bhakti or divine love is a realisation so profound that it is not possible to describe it adequately and exactly.

It is possible to describe the means to devotion, but not the sweetness of devotion itself. When it is impossible to describe the taste of apple to one who never tasted it, how can the joy of supreme love be communicated by words? Love is a feeling felt within the heart. When one is underneath the water he cannot speak. Similarly when one is drowned in the ocean of divine love, he is unable to speak.

The sixteen Sutras of the fourth chapter speak about the marks of devotion.

Nouns and pronouns, etc., are useful only for giving names to external objects or their qualities or expressing the actions or the relations of those qualities. Adjectives express the quality of an object. The verb expresses an action, the adverb the mode or time, etc., in relation to such action.

Speech deals with external objects. Prem or Bhakti or divine love is an internal emotion which does not originate from an external impulse coming from any external object. Therefore, speech or word is not capable of expressing it. The language of tears or sighs can express to some extent the inner state of the devotee.

This is to be felt by the devotee himself. Even in the worldly parlance it is impossible to describe the taste of sugar-candy to one who has not eaten sugar-candy, the nature of sexual happiness to one who has not enjoyed it, and the nature of sun and sun-light to a blind man. Hence the term *'Anirvachaniyam'* is used here.

मूकास्वादनवत् ॥५२॥

### Sutra 52. Mukasvadanavat.

*Just as the taste of a dumb man.*

मूकास्वादनवत् Muka-asvadanavat: like the taste of a dumb-man, like the dumb man's experience of a tasty thing.

The nature of love is as indescribable as the taste of a dumb person. It is like the dainty dish tasted by a dumb person.

Direct experience of divine love is something which is produced without the help of any external stimulus. It is a vision of truth or God which transforms the being of the devotee. It is not a thrill. It is not ordinary self-forgetfulness. The devotee feels the Lord's touch within the heart.

The dumb man will reveal his experience through smile. He may dance and jump with joy.

Saints try to describe the experience of divine love. They say, "It tastes like a palatable dish, a delicious fruit,

sweet syrup, celestial manna, sugar-candy, powdered
sugar-candy, honey, *Panchamritam*, sweet jam."

प्रकाशते क्वापि पात्रे ॥५३॥

**Sutra 53. Prakasate kvapi patre.**

*But (that love of devotion manifests itself in a fit recep-
tacle) in a qualified person only at some place or time.*

तत् That: love; क्वापि Kvapi: some; at any place and
time, where everything is favourable to its appearance, fit;
पात्रे Patre: receptacle in a fit recipient; प्रकाशते Prakasate:
is manifested, is revealed.

What will avail, then, on association with the saints if
the devotion or love is inexpressible in words and conse-
quently incommunicable from person to person? To this
the answer is that the operation of devotion or love is
telepathic and not through any grosser medium.

To some who are deserving, it can be revealed.

Rays of divine love radiate through the eyes of a saint
at every pore of his body.

The methods to be adopted for acquiring such fitness
have been explained before namely, *Vishayatyaga, san-
gatyaga, avyavritabhajan, bhagavat gunasravana kirtan, etc.*

"Kvapai" : somewhere, at some time. The extreme
rarity of such individuals is here indicated. Out of many
millions one will fit to receive the Lord's grace. A saint
also comes to the earth only very, very rarely. Many
generations may pass before one such person takes his
birth.

The current of Prem or spiritual aura passes by itself
from the teacher to the fit disciple. There is telepathic
transference or communication between the teacher and
disciple. The disciple should be a fit subject to receive the

light. The seed will sprout only in a well prepared ground.
There is Saktisanchar through Sankalpa ground. There is
*Shaktisanchar* through Sankalpa or sight by the teacher in
the student.

गुणरहितं कामनारहितं प्रतिक्षणवर्धमानमविच्छिन्नम् सूक्ष्मतरमनु-
भवरूपम् ॥५४॥

**Sutra 54. Gunarahitam kamanarahitam pratikshana-
vardhamanamavicchinnam sukshmataramanubhavarupam.**

*It (divine love) is devoid of all attributes, devoid of all
desires, expanding every moment, continuous, most subtle
and of the nature of inner experience.*

गुणरहितं Gunarahitam: devoid of all attributes;
कामनारहितं Kamanarahitam: bereft of desire; प्रतिक्षणवर्धमानम्
Pratikshana-vardhamanam: expanding every moment;
अविच्छिन्नम् Avichchinnam: of ceaseless flow; सूक्ष्मतरम्
Sukshmataram: extremely subtle; अनुभवरूपम्
Anubhavarupam: of the form of feeling, of the nature of
inner experiences.

The divine love grows in volume and intensity at every
moment. It has a ceaseless flow. It is of the form of subtler
feeling.

Even *Sattvic Bhakti* is far below the true Bhakti when
one loves God for love's sake.

Bhakti practised in order to get away from ills or to
attain certain desire is not genuine Bhakti.

It is impossible for the ordinary human mind to have
any conception of this exalted divine love. It is different
from the grosser love for things of this world.

Bhakti is realisable by intuition alone. Though Bhakti

is beyond speech and intellect, it can be directly intuited when you contact with God in your innermost being.

Attributes reside in matter and describe one or other aspect of relativity, while divine love is beyond matter and relativity.

You can grasp with the mind and describe in language an object only through its properties. Devotion is devoid of these and so it cannot be described in words.

Divine love is infinite. Worldly love is often cut short. It is broken. It decreases or wanes or declines like the waning moon. Newer interests, fresher attractions have to be resorted to, in order to keep earthly love alone. A girl loves her parents first. This love gets decreased when she gets married. She loves her husband more. When she begets a son, she loves her son more then her husband. This is mundane love. But divine love grows deeper and deeper every moment. It expands like the waxing moon. It ascends higher and higher like the Himalayan range.

Worldly love is divisible. A man who has six children distributes his love among all the six. But devotion to the Lord is not divisible.

Divine Love seeks no return, grows from more to more every moment, knows no break, is subtler than the subtlest and is of the nature of pure, inner experience. It is beyond the pale of the three Gunas. It is a spontaneous outpouring of the heart.

Divine Love is not dependent on youth, beauty, wealth, or virtue. It is not tainted by self-interest. There is no thought of personal gain here. It is very subtle, very soft, very slender, very remote. It is the fountain of all sweetness. It is unvaried in sweetness. It is constant. It is the hardest of all. It is brimful or full. It is unwavering and sublime. It unites the devotee with the Lord and makes him an embodiment of bliss.

The divine current of love begins to flow only when one goes beyond the influence of the three Gunas.

At first there is a glimpse of the Lord. Gradually the devotee becomes identified with the Lord.

"Anu" is a prefix expressing nearness, participation, conformity. Love or Ananda exists. It is Bhava. The individual soul participates in it. His nearness to it, his conforming himself to its nature, his participation of it, is indicated by the prefix "Anu".

There is God's love. The individual soul participates in this love. That is the Anubhava. So divine love is *Anubhavarupam*.

Ordinary emotions depend on certain external causes and objects and are therefore transitory. The emotion vanishes when the cause or object is removed. One also becomes satisfied in a short time by sense enjoyments. One can never become satiated with devotion or divine love. It can be experienced for all times. Devotion is independent of causes. Its content is a perennial fountain of eternal bliss. Therefore, it becomes more and more enjoyable as it deepens, as it strengthens in course of time.

It (love) is of the form of a very, very subtle, unbroken feeling or experience that develops in volume and intensity at every moment and is free from the three Gunas and desires.

It is very, very subtle. So the term *'Sukshmataram'* is used. It always grows and increases. There is always waxing. The play of Gunas has no place here. Sensual desires cannot exist when this unbroken love operates.

Whatever the mind wants can be had in God. His one attribute, *ananta* (infinite), embraces everything.

The next Sutra speaks about the effects of such
*Anubhava* or inner experience.

तत्प्राप्य तदेवावलोकयति तदेव श्रृणोति तदेव भाषयति तदेव
चिन्तयति ॥५५॥

**Sutra 55. Tatprapya tadevavalokayati tadeva srinoti tadeva
bhashtyati tadeva chintayati.**

*Having once attained that, (the devotee) sees only his
object of devotion, hears only about Him, speaks only about
Him, thinks only of Him.*

तत् Tat: that, love, devotion, inner experience, object
of love; प्राप्य Prapya: having attained; तत् Tat: that; एव
Eva: alone; अवलोकयति Avalokayati: sees; तत् Tat: that; एव
Eva: alone: श्रृणोति Srinoti: hears; तत् Tat: that; एव Eva:
alone; भाषयति Bhashayati: speaks; तत् Tat: that; एव Eva:
alone; चिन्तयति Chintayati: ponders over.

Attaining this love, the devotee sees nothing but love,
hears only about love, speaks only of love and thinks of
love alone.

Man first loves God with an object. Then by a transference of interest he loves God for love's sake, without
any object, for the sake of God who is an embodiment of
love.

Just as a river loses its individuality when it joins the
ocean, the devotee loses his egoism or individuality when
he becomes one with the Lord. Then he sees himself and
all the rest of the world as the Lord Himself, as inseparable part of that universal love.

This divine love is all-possessing. The devotee has no

other interest in life. To him the entire universe is a mirror which reflects the Lord and the Lord alone.

He has neither friends, nor enemies; he has no country, no nationality, no caste, no special states. The whole world is his home. The whole world is the body of the Lord. He is dumb to any talk other than the praises of the Lord. His ears are deaf for anything other than the Leelas of the Lord. His mind is ever absorbed in the Lord and oblivious of the World.

A Gopi expresses her experience thus: "In whichever direction I look, I find the landscape full of Shyama, dark blue. The water of the Yamuna is dark. The bowers and groves are dark. The letters of the Vedas are dark."

He sees only the Lord in everything. The devotee looks only at the Lord. He hears only the Lord. He thinks only of the Lord. How can he be conscious of the external universe?

A Devotee who undergoes the discipline mentioned above (Sutras 46-49) sees the whole world as a manifestation of God. Every one of his activities, physical and mental, will be an expression of his devotion to the Lord.

In the next Sutra, Narada speaks of devotees who are still under the influence of Guans.

# SECONDARY DEVOTION

## गौणी त्रिधा गुणभेदादार्तादि भेदाद्वा ॥५६॥

### Sutra 56. Gauni tridha gunabhedadartadibhedadva.

*Secondary devotion is of three kinds according to the qualities, Sattva, Rajas and Tamas and according to the distinction of the aspirants, the afflicted, the seeker after knowledge, the self-interested.*

गौणी Gauni: secondary (Bhakti); त्रिधा Tridha: threefold; गुणभेदात् Guna-bhedat: according to the difference of the qualities, viz., Sattva, Rajas and Tamas; आर्तादि भेदात् Artadi bhedat: according to the distinction of the worshippers as the afflicted, the seeker after knowledge, the self-interested; वा Va: or.

The primary type of devotion (*Ahaituki* or unmotivated) through which the devotee attains his beloved Lord has been discussed in the previous Sutras. Now the secondary Bhakti is being discussed.

Worship done without selfishness is Sattvic devotion. Worship done for getting power and wealth is Rajasic devotion. Worship done to injure others is Tamasic devotion.

Sattva is stainless like the crystal (*Sphatikamani*). Sattva lays for one the trap of happiness and knowledge. Sattva is a golden fetter. A Sattvic man compares himself with others and rejoices in his excellence. He is puffed up with his knowledge. His heart is filled with pride when he thinks that he has more comforts or more pleasant experiences.

He thinks "I am happy. I am wise" and so he is bound. This attachment to happiness is an illusion.

If you trust in God there is no need for asking anything from Him. He gives you anything you want without asking.

*Gauna-bhakti* or secondary devotion culminates in *Mukhyabhakti*, primary devotion, which is one continuous, unbroken stream of love for God and which is devoid of all taints.

The second classification is based on the difference in the motives that impel the devotee. Of the four varieties of devotees mentioned in the Gita, chapter VII-6, the first three are varieties of *Gauna Bhakti*. The fourth denotes *Mukhyabhakti* in which the devotee loves God and God alone. It is love for love's sake.

Draupadi and Gajendra were arta *bhaktas*. They were in distress. Uddhava was a *Jijnasu bhakta*. Dhruva was an *artarta bhakta*. He wanted dominion.

उत्तरस्मादुत्तरस्मात् पूर्वपूर्वा श्रेयाय भवति ॥५७॥

**Sutra 57. Uttarasmaduttarasmat purvapurva sreyaya bhavati.**

*Each preceding one (kind of devotion) is more conducive to the highest good then the one succeeding it.*

उत्तरस्मादुत्तरस्मात् Uttarasmaduttarasmat: than each succeeding one; पूर्वपूर्वा Purva purva: each preceding one; श्रेयाय Sreyaya: for the better, for the sake of the highest good; भवति Bhavati: is, works.

The first is better and more fruitful than the second and the second is better and more fruitful than the third in both the divisions.

The first of these conditions produces higher spiritual

good than the second, and the second is superior to the third.

Rajasic Bhakti practised in order to obtain power and wealth is better than Tamasic Bhakti which involves divine help to injure others. Sattvic Bhakti is still higher, for it only aspires to know God.

Sattva is harmony, peace, light. It is the highest state. The desire for pleasure and power (Rajas) is better than inertia (Tamas) which is equivalent to spiritual death. A devotee should carefully watch his mind and note which of these conditions prevails in his mind. He should strive to increase Sattva by Satsanga, Japa, Kirtan, meditation, worship, etc.

According to the second classification *Arta Bhakti* (Bhakti of affliction) is higher. Here affliction does not refer to any misery due to worldly evil, but to distress due to the conscious separation from God. (See aphorism 19.)

The devotion practised by the seeker of truth (*jijnasu*) is better than that practised by the seeker of wealth (*Artharthi*) and better and more fruitful than both the types is the devotion of the afflicted and the distressed (*arta*). An *arta* alone makes a passionate, sincere and intense appeal to the Lord and gets help immediately. He wants relief at once. Draupadi and Gajendra are the examples.

An *arta* wants God and nothing else, because no one else can give relief to him. A *jijnasu* wants knowledge, not God. The *artharthi* does not want even knowledge. He wants wealth. Therefore, the *Arta* is the best of the whole lot. .

The Gopis were extremely miserable on account of separation from Lord Krishna. They were also *artas*. They prayed and sang. Then the Lord gave them His presence.

A Devotee who has intense *Vairagya* or dispassion never rests satisfied with anything less than the supreme God-realisation.

*Mukhya Bhakti* is superior to *Sattvic Bhakti* and *Para Bhakti* is superior to *Mukhya Bhakti*.

# BHAKTI EASY TO PRACTISE

## अन्यास्मात् सौलभ्यं भक्तौ ॥५८॥

**Sutra 58. Anyasmat saulabhyam bhaktau.**

*The practice of devotion is easier than other methods (in the attainment of salvation).*

भक्तौ Bhaktau: in devotion, with respect to divine love; अन्यास्मात् Anyasmat: than others, than any other; सौलभ्यं Saulabhyam: easy recognisability, cheapness, the nature of being easily obtained.

Bhakti is easier than any other way of approach to God.

Karma, Yoga, Jnana are the three other paths. Bhakti is the direct approach to the ideal through the heart. Love is natural to everybody.

The practice of devotion is the easiest of all forms of spiritual practice.

Karma, Yoga, Jnana are the three other paths. It is only a help to knowledge and devotion. It purifies the heart of the aspirants. Vedic rites can be performed only by wealthy people.

Yoga is beset with difficulties and dangers. The Yogi gets powers and misuses them and gets his downfall. It is very difficult to practise *Pratyahara, Pranayama,* etc.

The pursuit of knowledge is dry for some, while that of devotion is sweet and enjoyable. *Jnana Yoga* demands vast study, sharp and subtle intellect, bold understanding and gigantic will.

Bhakti can be practised under all conditions and by all alike, irrespective of age and sex.

Learning, austere penance, study of the Vedas, brilliant intellect are not needed for the attainment of Bhakti or devotion. What is wanted is constant and living remembrance of God, coupled with faith. That is the reason why the path of Bhakti is (*Saulabhyam*) available for every one.

Many people think very low of *Bhakti Yoga* and resort to Hatha Yoga, Kundalini Yoga, Raja Yoga without any qualification at all. They do not practise Yama and Niyama. They practise *Khechari Mudras,* etc., and Pranayama because they think they can move along the sky and perform miracles. Maya clouds their vision.

A Bhakta gets everything. He gets Siddhis, the grace of the Lord and His wonderful vision.

Thus Bhakti Yoga is the most accessible for all sorts of people.

## प्रमाणान्तरस्यानपेक्षत्वात् स्वयं प्रमाणत्वात् ॥५९॥

**Sutra 59. Pramanantarasyanapekshatvat svayam pramanatvat.**

*Because it (devotion, love) does not depend on any other proof, as it is proof of itself.*

प्रमाणान्तरस्य Pramanantarasya: of any proof other than itself; अनपेक्षत्वात् Anapekshatvat: because of non-dependence; स्वयं Svayam: itself, in itself; प्रमाणत्वात् Pramanatvat: being of the nature of proof, being evidence.

Because there is no need of any other evidence, as it is self-evident.

The proof of devotion is devotion itself. It requires no other proof. The devotee has direct experience of divine bliss when he is in communion with the Lord. There is no need of any external proof. It is not a thing to be verbally explained. A woman who experiences the joy of the marital state alone knows what it is like. She cannot explain it to an unmarried girl.

Proof is an instrument of correct knowledge. When one is enjoying a sweet mango fruit, he is not in need of additional proof of the sweetness of mango. He does not ask himself for a proof of that state. Even so there is no need of any proof for a devotee who is enjoying the divine bliss directly. He does not enter into logical discussions or intellectual gymnastics like a dry logician.

*"Pramana"* is proof. *"Antara"* is 'external'. *"Pramanantara"* is "external proof". According to the Mimamsakas there are six kinds of Pramanas viz., *Pratyaksham, Anumanam, Upamanam, Sabdam, Anupalabdhi and Arthapatti. Pratyaksham* is preception or direct apprehension by the senses. *Anumanam* is inference or the conclusion from given premises. *Upamanam* is the standard of comparison, that to which anything is compared. *Sabdam* is verbal authority (Vedas). *Anupalabdhi* is non-perception as proof of the non-existence of a thing. *Arthapatti* is a conclusion, inference, presumption that results from a fact that is known to be true or that has been accepted.

The Naiyayikas recognise only the first four. The Sankhyas accept only *Pratyaksha, Anumana* and *Sabda.*

All these other than the first i.e., Pratyaksha, are dependent upon something other than one's own direct experience. They may be taken to be external evidence or *Pramanantaram*. The Bhakti Marga does not want them. It deals with the direct recognition of the emotion of love.

When you feel hungry, you know it at once. You have direct experience. You do not listen to intellectual arguments about hunger to feel hungry. If some one says, "No, you are not hungry," you say, "I am hungry. I am an authority to say whether I am hungry or not. No one else can be the authority on this matter."

When you love your mother, wife, or child, you do not argue, you are not in need of any external proof. You are yourself the authority for this direct experience. That is why the Sutra says, *"Svayam Pramanaraupatvatcha."*

It does not require a second person to prove to one whether he is happy or miserable. It is not necessary to apply any inference to know it. Any amount of argument cannot convince one against one's own experience. Direct experience is the primary and infallible means of all valid knowledge.

शान्तिरूपात् परमानन्दरूपाच्च ॥६०॥

**Sutra 60. Santirupat paramanandarupachcha.**

*(The path of devotion is easy) because it (devotion) is of the nature of peace and supreme bliss.*

शान्तिरूपात् Santirupat: because of its being of the form of peace of mind; परमानन्दरूपात् Paramanandarupat: because of its being of the form of supreme bliss; च cha: and.

The devotee forgets everything, even himself. He truly lives only for God. He lives in God.

Honey gives sweetness at once to anyone who tastes it. Even so devotion bestows perfect peace and supreme bliss. This fact is self-evident. It admits of no further proof.

Love of God is experienced as *Santi* (peace) and *Paramananda* (supreme bliss).

लोकहानौ चिन्ता न कार्या निवेदितात्मलोकवेदत्वात् ॥६१॥

**Sutra 61. Lokahanau chinta na karya niveditatmalokavedatvat.**

*The Bhakta should feel no anxiety about worldly concerns, as he has consecrated himself, the world as well as the Vedas to the Lord.*

लोकहानौ Loka-hanau: with regard to the miseries of the world, in respect of social disorganisation: चिन्ता Chinta: anxiety, thought; na: not; कार्या Karya: should be cherished, is to be entertained; निवेदितात्मलोकवेदत्वात् Nivedita-atma-loka-vedatvat: on account of his having surrendered to the Lord his own Self, the worlds and the Vedas.

The devotee should not entertain any anxious thought about social disorganisation, as he has dedicated his self and customary and scriptural morality to the Lord.

The devotee need not worry if his affairs go wrong, because his self, worldly affairs and even the Vedas have been surrendered to the Lord. The devotee should have complete trust in God, even when they go the wrong way apparently. Really neither loss nor evil can touch him, because he is under the care and protection of a loving and Omnipotent Lord. He must take no notice of worldly gain or loss. He is not concerned with what he achieves in the world or what he loses.

The devotee has surrendered himself as well as his temporal and spiritual concerns to the Lord. Therefore, he should not worry about worldly losses. What need has he to worry about things of the world?

When the devotee has surrendered himself as well as his all to the Lord, the Lord removes all his anxieties. He takes away the mind of his devotee. How can he worry about the loss in the absence of the mind?

This Sutra does not advocate hardness of heart or indifference to human suffering. It does not condemn the charitable acts and philanthropic work of large-hearted people. It emphasises only one point — *Chinta-na-Karya* — No anxiety or worry is to be entertained.

The devotee has surrendered his Atma (intellect, mind and body), attachment to the world and also his reverence to the Vedas (discipline, rules, etc.) as *Nivedanam* to the Lord.

# BHAKTI AND SOCIAL CUSTOMS

न तत् सिद्धौ लोकव्यवंहारो हेयः किन्तु फल त्यागस्तत्
साधनंच कार्यमेव ॥६२॥

**Sutra 62. Na tat siddhau lokavyavaharo heyah kintu phala-tyagastat sadhanancha karyameva.**

*Till Bhakti is developed one must not neglect to observe social customs and ceremonies. One should surely perform them but only the fruits of all social activities are to be surrendered to the Lord.*

तत्सिद्धौ Tat Siddhau: for attaining it, in the development of devotion: लोकव्यवहारः Lokavyavaharah: social life, social custom and usage; न Na; not ; हेयः Heyah: to be neglected; किन्तु Kintu: but; फल त्यागः Phala-tyaga: renunciation of the fruits of actions: तत्साधनम् Tatsadhanam: means helpful to it, its performance च Cha: and कार्यम् Karyam: must be performed: एव Eva: certainly.

So long as this Bhakti is not achieved, the ordinary way of life should not given up but renunciation of the desire for reward of actions and discipline preparatory to it should be persistently practised. Conscious efforts must be made steadily in the form of selfless work and discipline of the mind.

On the attainment of Bhakti, or even for the attainment of it, life in the society should not be given up. All righteous activities must be continued. Only the fruits of such actions must be relinquished. Sri Vasishtha, Vyasa,

Sankara, Lord Jesus, Lord Buddha and others have been the most active benefactors of mankind.

"*Loka-vyavahara*" : You eat and drink. You breathe. You are doing something. Therefore, you have no excuse to give up the duties entrusted to you. This is the meaning of "*Loka-Vyavahara.*"

स्त्रीधननास्तिकवैरिचरित्रं न श्रवणीयम् ॥६३॥

**Sutra 63. Stree dhana nastika vairi charitram na sravaniyam.**

*Stories or description of women, wealth, atheists or enemy should not be listened to.*

स्त्रीधननास्तिकवैरिचरित्रं Stree – Dhana – Nastika – Vairi charitram: descriptions or the behaviour or conduct of women, wealth and ungodly persons (who deny the authority of the Vedas and the existence of God) and of enemies: न na: not; श्रवणीयम् Sravaniyam: should be listened to.

In this and the following as well as in the 73rd, 74th, 43rd, 44th and 45th aphorisms, the obstacles to the development of devotion have been enumerated.

Such occasions decrease spirituality in the devotee and render him incapable of further progress.

He whose mind is engrossed in thoughts of women can never meditate on God. The thought of woman arouses passion. Passion is the greatest obstacle in the path of God-realisation.

The thought of wealth generates greed. Thought of an atheist and company of an atheist causes disbelief in God. Thought of the enemy generates anger. Therefore, stories of these four should never be heard.

Talks about women disturb the mind and excite passion. In the Narada Parivrajak Upanishad it is said that the seeker should not look even at the picture of a woman. Talks of wealthy persons will induce luxury in the aspirant. The acts of atheists will destroy the conviction of God.

अभिमानदंभादिकं त्याज्यम् ॥६४॥

**Sutra 64. Abhimanadambhadikam tyajyam.**

*Egoism, hypocrisy and other vices should be given up.*

अभिमानदंभादिकं Abhimanadambhadikam; egoism, hypocrisy and other vices; त्याज्यम् Tyajyam: should be totally annihilated.

It is difficult to give up these evil traits by effort. The proper remedy is to divert their courses. Cultivation of the opposite virtues, viz., humility, modesty, simplicity will easily remove them.

Egoism creates a barrier between man and man. An egoistic man separates himself from others.

Hypocrisy is pretending to be what one really is not. A hypocrite feigns or pretends. He pretends to be a pious devotee. He pretends to possess virtues which he does not actually possess. He puts on a false appearance.

*"Aadikam"*, etc. By adding, etc., after Abhimana and Dambha, Devarishi Narada has made an indirect reference to the other evils coming under the head of the demoniacal qualities. Therefore, all the demoniacal traits should be given up by the devotee.

तदर्पिताखिलाचारः सन् कामक्रोधाभिमानादि तस्मिन्नेव<br>करणीयम् ॥६५॥

**Sutra 65. Tadarpitakhilacharah san kamakrodhabhimanadi Tasminneva karaniyam.**

*Having once dedicated all activities to God, he (the devotee) should show (if at all) his desire, anger, egoism, etc., only to Him.*

तदर्पिताखिलाचारः Tadarpita-akhila-acharah: one who has dedicated all activities to Him; सन् San: being; कामक्रोधाभिमानादि Kama-krodha-abhimana-adikam: desire, anger, egoism, etc.; तस्मिन् tasmin: with reference to Him; एव eva: alone करणीयम् Karaniyam: should be employed or shown or cherished.

This refers to the process of sublimating every one of our emotions and directing it towards God. All our actions internal and external should become a sacred offering unto the Lord. Then alone will they be transmuted and welded into pure devotion or Bhakti.

If the devotee is angry, he is angry with his beloved; if he is proud, he is proud of Lord; if he has a desire, Lord alone is the object of that desire. The persistent thought of the Lord, whether in love or even hate, transforms the heart into a sacred shrine. Ravana hated Lord Rama. He attained a high state after his death because his mind dwelt constantly on the Lord.

Just as the Lord is the object of love of his devotee even so is He the object of the latter's desire, anger, etc. As no one else exists in the eyes of the devotee except the Lord, who else will become the object of these last emotions or impulses?

Emotions which stand as obstacles in the spiritual path are changed into aids when directed towards God. Passion, anger, etc., get absorbed in the Lord.

The devotee who entirely depends on God can make Him the object of his passion, anger and pride.

On one occasion Sri Radha got angry with Sri Krishna on account of some mischievous pranks played by Him. She said to her companions, "Do not mention His Name to me. I shall never meet Him again, so long as I live. Let not Sri Krishna come in my presence. Do not allow Him to enter the gate. How can people who indulge in hypocrisy like Him be trusted?"

Anger may be directed towards the obstacles to devotion. It will then take the form of dispassion and renunciation. When one directs his anger against his own evil qualities, he is only purifying himself. The evil impressions will vanish. The Sattvic nature will fully manifest.

त्रिरूपभंगपूर्वकं नित्यदास्यनित्यकान्ताभजनात्मकं प्रेम कार्यं
प्रेमैव कार्यम् ॥६६॥

**Sutra 66. Trirupabhangapurvakam   nityadasyanityakanta-bhajanatmakam premakaryam premaiva karyam.**

*Love and love alone such as that of a devoted servant or a wife, which transcends the three forms mentioned before (in Sutra 56) should be practised.*

त्रिरूपभंगपूर्वकं Trirupa-bhanga-purvakam: transcending the triple form, having broken through the three forms (vide Sutra 56) of secondary devotion modified by the three qualites Sattva, Rajas and Tamas; नित्यदास्यनित्यकान्ताभजनात्मकं Nityadasya-nityakantabhajanat-makam: consisting of constant loving service such as that of a devoted servant or wife; प्रेम Prema: love; कार्यम् Karyam: should be practisecd; प्रेम Prema: love; एव Eva: alone; कार्यम् Karyam: should be practised.

Devotion or Bhakti which seeks to serve and love without any motive whatsoever, which has risen above the triad of lover, love and the loved, should always be the ideal of a devotee.

The highest form of divine love or devotion is the feeling of the lover, the art of loving and the object of love merged into one.

Dissolve the triple consciousness, namely, the worshipper, the object of worship and the act of worship. Cultivate that love alone in the form of constant service of the Lord *(Dasya Bhava)* or constant devotion to the Lord like that of devoted wife *(Kantabhava)*.

A Loyal servant or devoted wife does not expect any return or even gratitude from the master or the husband for all the services that are rendered as a mere offering of love. Even so the devotee sees only God in every creature. All his activities will therefore take the form of an offering of pure love to the Lord without any selfish motive or even recognition from Him. He loves because he cannot help loving God.

Tirutonda Nayanar had *Nitya Dasya bhava*. The Gopis of Brindavan, Andal and Mira had *Nitya Knata Bhava*.

## भक्ता एकान्तिनो मुख्याः ॥६७॥

### Sutra 67. Bhakta ekantino mukhyah.

*Those who have one-pointed devotion to God for His own sake are primary.*

एकान्तिनः Ekantinah: single hearted, those who possess one-pointed devotion to the Lord for His own sake, those whose only object of love is God; भक्ताः Bhakta: devotees; मुख्याः Mukhyaha: are primary.

Bhaktas who are exclusively attached or devoted to the Lord are the best of His devotees.

The body, mind, wealth and everything else become

the property of God. He lives in the world as His instrument. His mind is absorbed in God. His eyes see the Lord everywhere and at every time.

The Lord has settled in the eyes of the devotee. No one can enter his eyes now. Even sleep has no access there.

The fifth and the last chapter begins with this Sutra. In this chapter a description of one who has attained this stage of devotion known as *Mukhya bhakti* or primary devotion is given. The word *Mukhya* distinguished the devotion of this supreme stage from the *Gauna* or secondary devotion mentioned in the 56 Sutra.

He who has attained this primary Bhakti or absolute state of devotion is called a Bhagavata or Sant (Saint). This primary devotion is not tinged with any worldliness or selfishness. The devotee does not long even for Mukti. He does not love God as a means to an end.

A description of the nature of a true Bhakta is given in Bhagavata (XI.14.14), "He who has resigned his mind to me, does not seek after the position of Brahma or that of Indra, or an emperor's throne or lordship over Patala, or the attainment of Yogic powers, or even Moksha from which there is no returning; for he desires nothing but Myself." Sucha one was Uddhava. Of him the Lord says, "Neither Brahma, nor Sankara, nor Samkarshana, nor Sri Devi, nor my own self is so very dear to me as you are.

"Just as fire growing into a flame turns all fuel to ashes, so devotion to Me, O Uddhava, burns out all sins.

"Neither Yoga, nor Sankhya, nor righteous duties, nor the study of the Vedas, nor Tapas, nor liberal gifts propitiate me so well as the well-developed and unswerving devotion to me. I am won only through undivided Bhakti and faith. I am the beloved Atman of the righteous.

Devotion to me purifies even such outcaste as that eat dog's flesh and saves them from births.

"People do not accept fellowship in residence with Me, prosperity equal to Mine, nearness to Me, appearance in the same forms as I appear, or even unification with Me, even when these are offered to them; they only pray for employment in My service. It is this link of devotion which has been said to be the absolute, by which, overcoming attachment to the world, they become fit for attaining My nature."

That is the nature of *Ekanata Bhakti*. Ekanta means "having only one end." That end is to be in the presence of the Lord always and ever doing service to Him. Such devotees have only one thought of God.

कण्ठावरोधरोमाञ्चाश्रुभिः परस्परं लपमानाः पावयन्ति कुलानि
पृथिवीं च ॥६८॥

**Sutra 68. Kanthavarodharomanchasrubhih parasparam lapamanah pavayanti kulani prithivim cha.**

*Conversing with one another with a choking voice, with hairs standing on end, with tears flowing from their eyes, they purify their families as well as the earth (the land which gave birth to them).*

कण्ठावरोधरोमाञ्चाश्रुभिः Kantha-varodha-romanch-asrubhih: with choking of voice, hairs standing on end and tears (flowing from the eyes); परस्परम् Parasparam: with one another: amongst themselves; लपमानाः Lapamanah: conversing; कुलानि Kulani: families: clans; पृथिवीम्म Prithivim: the earth; च cha: and: पावयन्ति pavayanti: purifying.

In the Gita, X-9, Lord Krishna says, "Having their minds fixed upon Me and their life directed to Me, enlightening one another, and constantly talking about Me, My devotees become satisfied and delighted."

Talking of Bhakti to one another in faltering tone, attended with thrill and tears of joy, they sanctify their race and the wide earth.

The spirits of the ancestors of the devotees feel gratified and purified by the devotion of their descendents.

When there is a congregational prayer, when devotees

meet together and do kirtan and common meditation, they generate a spiritual current or force which inspires and purifies the hearts of many. The whole atmosphere of that place gets purified and is surcharged with currents of Divine Love.

The scriptures say, "Holy is the family and blessed the mother, nay, the earth itself is fortunate through him whose mind is absorbed in the Supreme Brahman, the ocean of infinite knowledge and bliss."

Lord Hari, said, "I do not dwell exclusively in Vaikuntha nor in the hearts of Yogis, but, O Narada, I am verily present in my splendour, where my devotees sing of me."

Choking voice, hairs standing on end and tears flowing from the eyes are external marks of the internal emotion. They express intensity of feeling. This feeling is Prem or divine love. He who has such a Prem can have direct communion with the Lord.

The greater the Bhakti is, the greater the orbit of the spiritual influence. The greatest of them are the light of the whole universe. Even if they live in caves, the spiritual waves generated by their devotion will spread over the entire universe and find an echo in all pure hearts ready to receive them.

The emotion of a devotee is *Vibhava* or *Anubhava* or *Bhava*. When the devotee is enjoying divine Bliss, his Prem is mixed up with Rasa (taste or sentiment).

The emotion of a devotee is *Vibhava* or *Anubhava* or *Vyabhichari bhava*. Vibhava is of two kinds, *Alambana* and *Uddipana*.

*Alambana Vibhava* is the ecstasy which the devotee expresses on account of an external impulse. The mere sight of a dark cloud will make the devotee see Lord Krishna in it. He will lose all consciousness of the world. *Vibhava* means having no consciousness of the external world. *Alambana* is "taking hold." The external phenomena have taken hold of the devotee.

In *Uddipana Vibhava* the devotee hears the flute played by Lord Krishna. The music generates *Vibhava*. *Uddipana* means illuminating.

After *Alambana, Uddipana* comes. *Anubhava* is the third stage. The devotee joins the company of the celestials surrounding the Lord. He is actually in Brindavan at that time. He takes part in dancing, *singing, etc. All the sentiments namely Rati, Hasya, Utsaha, Daya, Jugupsa, Soka* and *Vismaya* manifest in him. They will be shown in the form of glances, perspiration, etc.

In *Anubhava* there are external signs such as hairs standing on end, tears flowing from the eyes, etc. These are called *Sattvic Anubhava. Anubhava* is the primary mood, *Vyabhichari Bhav* is a secondary mood.

There are nine primary bhavas which are accompanied by secondary Bhavas. Wonder *(Vismaya)*, lifting of the eyes, opening of the lips, etc., are the *Vyabhichari Bhavas*.

"Pavayanti". The devotees purify. "Kulani"; their families. "Prithivim cha"; also the world. Wherever they go, they radiate love and joy, they dispel fear and ignorance, they give new life and fresh life to the despondent; they inspire and elevate those who come to them. It is in this way that they purify.

Purification means removal of sin and ignorance. The very presence of the great devotees removes sorrow and suffering and ignorance, the root cause of sin and misery. In this way they purify this earth.

They get *Svarabhanga* (choking of the voice) when there is ebullition of divine prem in the heart, *Pulak* (horripilation or standing of hair on ends) and *Asrupat* (tears in the eyes). God lives in the tears of a devotee.

The next two Sutras elaborate this point still further.

तीर्थींकुर्वन्ति तिर्थानि सुकर्मीं कुर्वन्ति कर्माणि
सच्छास्त्रीकुर्वन्ति शास्त्राणि ॥६९॥

**Sutra 69. Tirthikurvanti tirthani sukarmi-kurvanti karmani sacchastrikurvanti sastrani.**

*They (such devotees) impart sanctity to places of pilgrimage; render actions righteous and good and give spiritual authority to scriptures.*

तिर्थानि Tirthani: holy places; तीर्थींकुर्वन्ति Tirthikurvanti: make holy places; कर्माणि Karmani: actions; सुकर्मीं कुर्वन्ति Sukarmikurvanti: make meritorious actions; शास्त्राणि Sastrani: scriptures; सच्छास्त्रीकुर्वन्ति Sat-sastrikurvanti: make authoritative; make sacred scripture.

The devotees turn ordinary bathing places into sacred places of purification, ordinary acts into pious deeds and words of instructions into holy texts.

Their presence adds holiness to the place where they live. Their thoughts are dynamic. Their thoughts transform their environments infusing them with peace and joy.

We do not know of any one who has become a saint by reading Shakespeare, Herbert Spencer, Milton, Goldsmith or Shelly, but there are thousands who have adopted a new divine life by studying the Gita, the Upanishads, "Wisdom of Siva," "Mind, Its Mysteries and Control", the Bible and the Noble eightfold Path and other such books and writings. Each time these books are studied by a man, he invests them with a new power capable of transforming the heart of him.

Jayaram studied practice of Yoga and became Swami Paramananda, 'Madi' studied the Ten Upanishads and became Swami Satchidananda, Vaidyanathan studied spiritual lessons and became Swami Narayana.

Goddess Ganga was propitiated by the austere penance of King Bhagiratha. She appeared before Bhagiratha and said, "All the sinners of this world will wash their sins and purify themselves by immersing their sinful bodies in my holy waters. Where shall I wash the immense store of sins they deposit in my watery body?"

Bhagiratha replied, "O sacred Mother! Holy saints will bathe in the Ganga and purge you of all your sins, because Lord Vishnu, the dispeller of all sins, dwells in their heart."

Buddha Gaya, Jerusalem and Mecca have all been regarded sacred only on account of their being respectively associated with Buddha, Jesus and Muhammad.

Brindavana and Mathura are sacred because of Lord Krishna. Ayodhya is holy because of Lord Rama. Naimisaranya is still visited by thousands of pilgrims on every New Moon day, because many Rishis of olden days dwelt there.

It is the Saint that constitutes the real Tirtha.

That which enables a man to cross over an obstacle, such as a boat in a river, is a Tirtha.

The stones on which they sat, the paths on which they have trodden, the villages through which they have passed, the lakes in which they have taken baths, the trees under which they have taken their food are sanctified. Their names are even now associated with these places and objects. Guru Nanak's name is linked with Panchasahab near Taxila. His fingers are shown in the Kund. Bodhi Tree in Gaya is associated with Lord Buddha. Hathiaharan tank near Sitapur is associated with Sri Rama. There are so many Hanuman Kunds, Sita Kunds and Lakshman Kunds in various places of pilgrimage.

तन्मयाः ॥७० ॥

### Sutra 70. Tanmayah.

*(For) They are full of Him.*

तन्मयाः Tanmayah: full of that; filled with the presence of God; merged or absorbed in Him.

In and around them they realised the presence of God everywhere and at all times.

Every one of those mentioned in the last Sutra is filled with the spirit of saints and through that with the spirit of the Lord Himself.

They have emptied themselves so completely that they entirely live in God. The lives of God-intoxicated devotees like Prahlada bear witness to this.

Just as river falling into the ocean becomes one with the ocean, even so the devotee having offered his body, mind, intellect, egoism and all at the feet of his beloved Lord becomes one with Him.

*"Sarvam Vishnumayam Jagat"* — "the whole world is full of Vishnu." This experience is described in the Gita, Ch. VII-19. "At the close of many births, the man full of wisdom cometh unto Me." "Vasudeva is all" saith he, the Mahatma, "Very difficult to find." This is grand realisation. The devotee is full of divine ecstasy.

## मोदन्ते पितरो नृत्यन्ति देवताः सनाथाः चेयं भूर्भवति ॥७१॥

**Sutra 71. Modante pitaro nrityanti devatah sanathah cheyam bhurbhavati.**

*(On the advent of a devotee) their forefathers rejoice, the Gods dance in joy and this earth gets a saviour.*

पितरः Pitarah: the departed ancestors, forefathers; मोदन्ते Modante: rejoice; देवताः Devatah: Gods, celestials; नृत्यन्ति Nrityanti: dance in joy; इयम् Iyam: this; भूः Bhu: earth; सनाथाः Sanathah: possessing a saviour; च cha: and; भवति Bhavati: becomes.

This earth is happy in their care. This earth finds in them its protectors or guardians. The earth is blessed by them.

The manes of forefathers, the spirits of the ancestors of the devotees of God feel the spiritual influence generated by the devotional practices of their descendents living on the earth. They rejoice over the devotional state of their descendents.

The earth feels the effect of our good and evil actions. It is a living, breathing, conscious entity for a saint with a spiritual eye or the eye of intuition. It is Bhu Devi or Mother earth full of life. It is Vishnu. It is Virat.

It is not a dead mass of matter of the lifeless debris of a nebula of a geologist. It is a living organism. It is very productive. Nothing is lifeless in the spiritual sense.

All the actions of a devotee are naturally conducive to the welfare of the world. So his advent is a happy augury for all.

The devotion of a devotee redeems a number of

generations (7 or 21) going before and coming after him. So the manes rejoice in the prospect of salvation.

The devotee puts many irreligious people on the path of devotion and Dharma. They perform charity, *Sraaddha, Tarpana,* and the five sacrifices. So the manes rejoice and the celestials dance in joy.

God gives Darshan to His devotee. The advent of a devotee is the precursor of the manifestation of the Lord. God manifests and destroys the Asuras or wicked men, the enemies of Gods. Therefore, Gods also dance in joy.

A devotee can help the *Pitris*. He can give them what they want. That is why the *pitris* rejoice on the advent of a devotee.

The Asuras will not be powerful when there are devotees on this earth. The earth will be having more men with divine qualities. The saints will convert diabolical men into divine beings with virtuous qualities. So the Devas dance in joy.

Saints radiate the current of love and peace. They disseminate the message of unity, love, peace and goodwill on this earth. They stop wars. They send their disciples to preach the gospel of love and peace. Therefore, this earth also rejoices. She gets a Natha or saviour.

The word *pitru* is used in the scriptures to denote not only living parents but also ancestors and permanent demigods known by the name *Agnisvatta* and others. The living parents also rejoice because their son will be honoured by the world after his attainment of God-realisation and will also save them from the wheel of birth and death. A devotee satisfies the danizens of all the three worlds.

Glory to saints and devotees!

नास्ति तेषु जातिविद्यारूपकुलधनक्रियादिभेदः ॥७२॥

**Sutra 72. Nasti teshu jatividyarupakuladhanakriyadi bhedah.**

*Among them (the devotees) there is no distinction based on caste, learning, beauty, family or birth, wealth, observance or profession and the like.*

तेषु Teshu: among them; जातिविद्यारूपकुलधनक्रियादिभेदः Jati-vidya-rupa-kula-dhana-kriyadi bheda: distinctions based on caste, learning, beauty, family, wealth, profession or observance and the rest: न Na: not; अस्ति Asti: exists like, there is.

In the Adhyatma Ramayana III-10-20, Sri Rama says, "Sex, birth, reputation, status, etc., do not confer any title to My worship; only devotion confers *Adhikara* or fitness, competence to do My worship.

However widely they may differ in other respects they are all alike in their pure and one-pointed love for God.

You should not judge a devotee or a saint by his birth or literary attainments. Kabir was a common weaver, Raidas a sweeper, Nandan an untouchable, Sadan, a butcher and yet they were great spiritual lights.

Visvamitra, Vyasa, Kavasa, Jabala, Mahidasa, Nammalvar, Kannapar, Tukaram and others were not Brahmins and yet they were great spiritual luminaries.

In devotion, caste, culture, physical appearance, birth, possessions, occupation, etc. Do not matter. He who has dedicated his all at the feet of the Lord and who constantly remembers Lord succeeds in attaining God-consciousness, no matter whether he is a Brahmin or a labourer, educated or uneducated, high-born or low-born, good-looking or ugly-looking, wealthy or poor.

Nisada was born in a low caste, Sabari was a rustic woman, Dhruva was an un-educated boy, Vidura and Sudama were very poor, Vibhishana was an ugly Rakshasa, Hanuman was a monkey, Jatayu was a bird, Gajendra was an elephant, the Gopis of Brindavan were not initiated into Vedic rites; but all of them attained God-realisation on account of their devotion and self-surrender.

The institution of Varnashrama is not condemned thereby. Bhakti and observance of the rules of Varnashrama are two separate things. They should not be confounded. Those who try to abolish the distinction in the name of Bhakti bring a slur on Bhakti. Therefore, devotees should never try to repudiate the authority of the scriptures. A devotee should not be treated with contempt on account of birth, etc. He should be judged by his devotion alone. Discrimination among devotees on grounds of caste, etc., has been declared an offence in Vaishnava scriptures.

A saint has risen above the three Gunas. He shines with the resplendence of divine illumination. He does not belong to one caste or community but to the whole humanity. That is the reason why there is no distinction of caste among the saints.

He has Para Vidya or Highest knowledge through direct God-realisation.

There is no distinction based upon appearance. Ashta Vakra had eight bends in his body. Agastya was a dwarf. Some may be clean shaven, others may have matted hair.

Kula: It means family and also race. Saints can come out of any race. St. Francis, Saint Catherine, and several others belong to the Western race. They were realised souls. There have been saints among Mussalmans. Kabir is another instance. Saintliness is not affected by distinctions between the rich and the poor, between one profession and another.

The discipline of surrender to the Lord does not demand the special qualifications of caste, birth, clan, sex, etc.

He who has devotion to the Lord is a Brahmin; he who has no faith in the Lord is a Sudra. An outcaste who has devotion and who is leading the life divine is far superior to a Brahman who is leading a vicious and abominable life.

The distinctions exist when a man is petty minded. These differences are created by the mind on account of Avidya. They all melt away when one gets Darshan of God or Atman. Love is a great leveller. It develops equal vision *(sama drishti)*. The advanced Bhakta becomes an *Ativarnashrami*. He goes beyond Varnashrama. The petty rules of society and man made laws cannot in any way bind him. He becomes absolutely free. He acts from his own view point by resting in God. His will and cosmic will have become one. His voice is the voice of God. His words are infallible. God speaks and acts through him. His ways are mysterious and incomprehensible. He takes food from anybody's hands. He lives with a cobbler or barber sometimes. He dines with a scavenger. Narasi Mehta did kirtan in the house of cobblers and scavengers. Orthodox Brahmins excommunicated him. Narasi Mehta attended a feast. The other Brahmanas ill-treated him and looked down on him with contempt. They all saw a cobbler on their sides. They understood the glory of Narasi Mehta and from that time onwards they began to adore him.

The reason for all saints being of equal eminence is mentioned in the next Sutra.

यतस्तदीयाः ॥७३॥

**Sutra 73. Yatastadiyah.**

*Because they are all His own.*

यतः Yatah: because, since; तदीयाः Tadiyah His own, belonging to Him, his.

For they all belong to Him.

Devotees belong to the Lord. They are the objects of His special love. He loves them for their sincere devotion and pure, virtuous life. Wealth, beauty, birth and culture are of no value without these two qualifications.

The devotees become embodiments of the Divine on account of their devotion. Therefore, they lose all sense of difference among themselves. No one recognises himself superior to the rest.

Devotees are equal in the sight of God because their devotion is the same in spite of apparent physical and social differences. They all belong to one group. To a devotee all the creatures in the world are the children of God or God Himself. Therefore, he sees them with equal vision or *Samadrishti*.

It is Lord Hari that has taken all these forms. The whole world is a manifestation of the Lord. *"Lokavattu Lila Kaivalyam"* — The whole world is the Lila of the Lord. God acts the parts of a professor, thief, prostitute, king, beggar, saint, rogue, genius, etc., in this big world-drama. He who has this understanding will have immense peace of mind. He will entertain no pride, *ghrina*, prejudice, intolerance or hatred towards anybody. One must be well-established in this Bhava. This Bhava will come and go away. Address everybody as Narayana and receive him with this Bhava. Your whole nature will be absolutely changed. It takes some time. You will have to struggle hard.

The next Sutra shows the way of how to make the mind offer itself completely to the Lord.

# INSTRUCTIONS TO DEVOTEES

## वादो नावलम्ब्यः ॥७४॥

**Sutra 74. Vado navalambyah.**

No controversy ought to be entered into.

वादः Vadah: dispute, vain discussion; न Na: Not; अवलम्ब्यः Avlambyah: should be undertaken, deserve to be entered into.

The devotee should never enter into argumentation. Vain discussion should be not undertaken by those who aspire to devotion, regarding the existence or attributes of God.

It has been pointed out in the Kathopanishad "How else can that be conceived except that it exists?"

It is not proper for one to enter into a controversy about God or other spiritual truths, or about comparative merits of different devotees.

Discussion is an intellectual luxury. In disputation the true spirit of enquiry vanishes and the joy of intellectual gymnastics or verbal warfare takes its place. The disputant takes delight in overthrowing his combatant through arguments and reasoning skill. But constructive reasoning is beneficial. A devotee should accept the truth as an established truth. Criticising the truth revealed in the sacred scriptures will end in disbelief.

The duty of a devotee is to love God and to realise God. Love is above reasoning. Argumentation is a great hindrance in the path of divine love or Bhakti. The duty of a devotee is to remember God every second. He need not know when the world was created, how it was created, why it was created. God will Himself reveal His truth to him whenever He wills.

Truth can never be realised through logical argument. Logical reasoning has no foundation or stability. Discussion produces unnecessary agitation in the mind. An agitated mind cannot grasp the truth.

Vain discussions, heated debates, wrangling, etc., end in hostility. When arguments fail people take to vituperation and fighting. Discussions entail wastage of energy and time. It is only mere verbal warfare and intellectual gymnastics (*Sabda vilas* and *Budhi vilas*). Nothing substantial is gained thereby. Everyone wants to show his pedantry, skill in argument, etc. Such a pundit cannot dream of getting Darshan of God. His is very far away from God. But a little divine talk can be had between people who are well united in hearts and who are free from pride for removing doubts and exchanging of ideas. This is salutory and beneficial.

बाहुल्यावकाशत्वादनियतत्वाच्च ॥७५॥

**Sutra 75. Bahulyavakasatvadaniyatatvaccha.**

*For there is plenty of room for diversity in views and no one view, based upon mere reason, is conclusive in itself.*

बाहुल्यावकाशत्वात् Bahulyavakasatvat: as there is room for diversity in views; अनियतत्वात् Aniyatatvat as no (view based on mere) reason is conclusive; च cha: and.

Vain discussion about God must not be encouraged because it can go on indefinitely and there will be still no certainty that it will arive at the truth. There are as many different view points as there are intelligent people.

Because it leads to endless arguments and leads to no certain conclusion.

Mere reasoning does not lead to realisation of God. Intellect is frail and finite. It is not able to grasp the Infinite. Even none of the great problems which affect human life has been conclusively solved by reasoning. Reasoning has only complicated the issues. Therefore, depend not on reason but depend on intuition which is ever infallible and correct.

In argumentation there is room for excess. It cannot determine anything. A conclusion arrived at through the process of reasoning is never the truth. God is attained not through argument but through the practice of devotion.

Every topic relating to God is capable of being argued out in a variety of ways. After all it is profitless discussion, for no argument is conclusive.

Anger rises to win victory over one's opponent. Vehemence is an unavoidable concomitant to argumentation or discussion. The ego is the cause for such vain discussion. How can there be perception of Truth so long as there is the ego?

Convincing reasons may be given to support two diametrically opposite views. Hence it does not follow that a view is true because it has the support from reason. What one man considers well-established by reason can easily be shaken by another more intelligent man. A lawyer uses his reason to prove even a false case to be true. Therefore, reason is often an unreliable guide.

Science provides many examples of exploded theories which were all once considered as well established through reason. No one view based on mere reasoning can be considered true once for all, because it can be proved to be untrue by better reason.

Vain discussion will go on indefinitely for days together. Yet people will not arrive at definite, positive conclusions. They will be fighting over words, roots, conjunctions and other grammatical points. God is certainly not in Vyakarana or logic or prosody. He is in the chambers of the heart. He is to be realised by purity and meditation and not by vain discussions. That is the reason why Lord Yama says to Nachiketas: "This Atman cannot be obtained by too much learning, or discussions or intelligence. He who gets the grace of God, who is chosen by the Lord as His favourite, gets the Darshan of Atman. He reveals to him His Nature. To him alone He manifests Himself." Therefore, give up hot discussion. Be humble. Do practical Sadhana.

Waste not time and energy in vain discussion.

भक्तिशास्त्राणि मननीयानि तद्बोधककर्माणि
करणीयानि ॥७६॥

**Sutra 76. Bhaktisastrani manananiyani tadbodhakakarmani karaniyani**

*(For the attainment of Bhakti) the teachings of scriptures that promote devotion should be constantly meditated upon and actions that rouse devotion should be performed.*

भक्तिशास्त्राणि Bhaktisastrani: treatises on devotion: मननीयानि Mananiyani: should be reflected upon तद्बोधककर्माणि Tadbodhakahkarmani: practices or acts that rouse devotion; करणीयानि Karaniyani: should be performed.

This Sutra is a supplement to Sutras 12, 14, 49 and 62. Sutras 12 and 14 refer to the Bhakta's attitude to study and spiritual practices, as well as social service, even after God-realisation. Sutras 49 and 62 refer to his attitude towards

the same before the dawn of devotion. Sutra 76 deals with
the same attitude during the stage of Mukhyabhakti. It is
clear that according to Narada a devotee does not give up
his spiritual practices or social service at any stage either
before or after realisation.

A devotee should study books which place before him
the ideals of devotion, the glory, the sweetness and the
Leelas of the Lord, the stories of saints and the practices
which help him to cultivate devotion. Devotion develops
by the study of such devotional scriptures.

The most important books are the Ramayana, Srimad
Bhagavatam, Narayaneeyam, the Gita, Vish-
nupurana, Adhyatma Ramayana, Tulasi Ramayana
(Ramacharitamanas), Vishnu Sahasranama, Sandilya
Sutras, Siva Purana, Devi Bhagavata, the Narada
Pancharatram, Practice of Bhakti Yoga, Essence of Bhakti
Yoga, Bhakti and Sankirtan, Bhakti-rasamritam, songs of
Alwars and Nayanars, Thevaram, Thiruvachakam,
Dasabodha, Tukaram's Abhanga, Jnaneshwari, Bhakti
Rasayana, Bhakti Rasamritasindhu, etc.

Every act that awakens the emotion of Bhakti must be
done. Keep the Puja room clean. Decorate the room. Burn
incense. Lit a lamp. Keep a clean seat. Bathe, wear clean
clothes. Apply Vibhuti or Bhasma and Kumkum on the
forehead. Wear Rudraksha or Tulasimala. All these
produce a benign influence on the mind and elevate the
mind also. They generate piety. They help to create the
necessary Bhava or feeling to invoke the deity that you
want to worship. The mind will be easily concentrated.

Practice of Sadachara or right conduct, Satsanga, Japa,
Smarana, Kirtana, prayer, worship, service to saints,
residence in places of pilgrimage, service to the poor and
the sick with divine Bhava, observances of Varnashrama

duties, offering of all actions and their fruits to the Lord, feeling the presence of the Lord in all beings, prostrations before the image and saints with all the eight parts of the body, renunciation of earthly enjoyments and wealth, charity, austerities and vows, practice of Ahimsa, Satyam and Brahmacharya—all these will help you to develop Bhakti.

You must not be lenient to the mind. You must rigidly follow all the rules prescribed in the Bhakti Sastras. Then alone will you evolve quickly. You must keep up a daily routine and programme and follow it strictly at all costs. If you are lenient to the mind, laziness will overtake you and you will procrastinate everything. That 'tomorrow' will never come. Even if you are of advanced age, think you are a college-student and follow the daily routine. The benefits of keeping up a daily routine and spiritual diary cannot be adequately described. This is the master-key for success in spiritual life.

सुखदुःखेच्छालाभादित्यक्ते काले प्रतीक्षमाणे क्षणार्धमपि व्यर्थं
न नेयम् ॥७७॥

**Sutra 77. Sukhaduhkhechchalabhadityakte kale pratikshamane kshanardhamapi vyartham na neyam.**

*One should not waste even half a second as all the time one has for meditation is the little that remains after what is spent in experiencing pleasure, pain, desire, gain, etc.*

सुखदुःखेच्छालाभादित्यक्ते Sukha-duhka-ichchalabhadi Tyakte: freed from pleasure, pain desire, gain, etc; काले Kale: in time; प्रतीक्षमाणे Pratikshyamane: when expectantly waited upon; क्षणार्धम् Kshanardham: half a moment; अपि Api: even; व्यर्थम् Vyartham: in vain; न Na: not; नेयम् Neyam: should be spent.

When one has given up pleasure, pain, desire, gain, etc., and is in a state of high expectancy, not even half a moment should be allowed to go in vain.

Time free from the sway of pleasure, pain, desire, profit or other worldly consideration is what every one seeks; therefore, even half a second should not be wasted. It should be spent in meditation on God.

Sukha is the quality of Sattva; Duhkha is the quality of Tamas. Ichcha is the quality of Rajas. When one has given up pleasure, pain, desire, etc., when one has given up the three Gunas, when he is waiting for the appearance of the Lord in the form in which He is requested by the devotee to appear, even half a second, should not be wasted. You should be extremely alert. You should not sleep. Within half a second, when your mind wanders, God may have come and gone without your noticing Him. Maya is very clever to take advantage of your carelessness even for half a second. You must be intensely watchful and vigilant. Be ever looking forward to God's appearance. This is high expectancy.

If the devotee is not vigilant and alert, Rajas and Tamas will pull him down from the height he has attained. Satan will easily find a loophole to enter and work mischief in him. If it is not cleaned by vigorous meditation every day, the mind will become impure like the brass vessel that is left uncleaned.

In youth you are enveloped in darkness. In adolescence you are carried away by lust and are given to sexual pleasure. In old age you groan under the burden of Samsara. Much time goes away in sleep, vain talk and idle gossip. A portion is spent in disease and suffering. Where is then the time for doing virtuous actions and divine contemplation? Life is uncertain. You will be carried away by death without a moments notice. Therefore, a wise man should be very careful in spending his time profitably in meditation. Time is most precious. Every second must be utilised in the service of God and Bhaktas and in meditation.

The next Sutra points out the necessity for such watchfulness, alertness and eternal vigilance. You are ever prone to yielding to the animal in you. You should be constantly fighting against evil tendencies such as Himsa, etc.

अहिंसासत्यशौचदयास्तिक्यादि चारित्र्याणि
परिपालनीयानि ॥७८॥

**Sutra 78. Ahimsasatyasouchadayastikyadi charitryani paripalaniyani.**

*Virtues like non-violence, truth, purity, compassion, faith in the Vedas and the existence of God, and other excellences of character should be strictly cultivated and protected.*

अहिंसासत्यशौचदयास्तिक्यादि चारित्र्याणि Ahimsa-satya-soucha-daya-astikya-adi charitryani: virtues like non-violence, truthfulness, purity, compassion, faith in the existence of God; परिपालनीयानि Paripalaniyani: should be strictly cultivated and protected.

Just as a plant in a garden is protected from insects, pests, etc., and is given suffcient manure for its growth, so also those virtues have to be protected and nourished. The food has already been mentioned in the previous Sutras, *"Avyavrita Bhajanat, Lokepi Bhagavat Guna sravana kirtanat"* Sutras 36 and 37.

*Ahimsa, satyam,* etc., are the Yamas (restraints). *Soucha, Santosha,* etc., are the Niyamas (observances). All these are the disciplines, without which no spiritual progress is possible.

*Daya* is active benevolence. It is the positive expression of love. Ahimsa is the negative expression of love.

In Sutra 76 Narada advises to perform actions which help the growth of devotion. In the present Sutra the devotee is asked to practise five special items of conduct.

In the practice of truth one must speak exactly what has been seen, heard or understood about a person or a thing. There should not be the least exaggeration or twisting. The speech should be truthful and sweet. Truth which leads to another's injury is not a desirable thing.

'Adi' etc. Narada intends to point to the other divine qualities such as courage, charity, control of senses, austerity, straightforwardness, humility, self-abnegation, tranquillity, freedom from wrath, tenderness of heart, sobriety, forgiveness, fortitude, etc.

The principles of Yama and Niyama of Patanjali Maharishi's Raja Yoga philosophy are embodied here. These are the very foundation of Yoga. Practice of these virtues purifies the heart and prepares the *Antahkarana* for the reception of divine light. Compassion softens the hard heart. *Satyam* purifies the heart. God is an embodiment of truth and He can be reached through the practice of truthfulness alone. Truth alone triumphs. If one is well-established in the practice of Ahimsa in thought, word, and deed, all other virtues will cling to him. Most of the vicious actions are done when one loses one's temper. Brahmacharya is the highest of all virtues. No Brahmacharya, no realisation. Without faith in God, neither Sadhana nor realisation is possible. Faith is the fundamental qualification of an aspirant. It is not blind faith. It is faith based on reason.

The mind is ever unsteady. How then to steady it? The next two Sutras teach how to fix the mind on God.

सर्वदा सर्वभावेन निश्चिन्तैर्भगवानेन भजनीयः ॥७९॥

**Sutra 79. Sarvada sarvabhavena nischintaih bhagavanena bhajaniyah.**

*The Lord alone should always be worshipped by one whole-heartedly free from all cares and anxieties.*

सर्वदा Sarvada: always; सर्वभावेन Sarva Bhavena: with the whole heart, through every aspect of life; निश्चिन्तैः Nischintaih: by those free from all cares and anxieties; भगवान् Bhagawan: the Lord; एव Eva: alone; भजनीयः Bhajaniya: should be worshipped.

"Chinta" : chinta means 'thinking', 'reflecting' 'being anxious about.'

Sarvabhavena: Bhava is mode of existence; in all their modes of existence, and in all their moods. In every aspect of life the devotee has only God-consciousness. In his attitude to the members of his family, to his friends who do good to him, to those who do evil, to his superiors and to his inferiors, in every relation that subsists between him and others he has only God-consciousness.

Bhagavan: He who has all glory, all power and all wisdom, i.e., the Lord.

Bhajanam: worshipping. 'Bhaj' literally means to 'share in', to obtain for oneself, to partake of. Bhakta is one who shares all the glory, power and knowledge with the Lord.

'Nischinta Bhajana' is complete concentration of the mind on God without a break at any time.

The Gita says: *"Tameva saranam gaccha sarva bhavena Bharata! Flee unto Him for shelter with all thy being, O Bharata!"* The whole heart, mind, intellect, Chitta and soul must be given to God without any reservation. Ch. XVIII-62. This is "Sarvabhavena". When you meditate, you must be free from thoughts of fear, worry or anxiety.

स कीर्त्यमानः शीघ्रमेवाविर्भवत्यनुभावयति भक्तान् ॥८०॥

**Sutra 80. Sa kirtyamanah sighramevavirbhavatyanubhavayati bhaktan.**

*Being thus invoked or glorified, He (the Lord) manifests Himself, and blesses His devotees with realisation.*

सः Sa: Me; कीर्त्यमानः Kirtyamanah: being invoked, being glorified; शीघ्रम् sighram: speedily; एव eva: surely; आविर्भवति avirbhavati: manifest; भक्तान् Bhaktan: devotees; revels Himself; अनुभावयति anubhavayati: makes (them) realise.

Lord Hari came out of the pillar in the form of Narasimha when Prahlada prayed with his full heart, "Sarva-bhavena". Prahlada said to his father: "My Narayana is in your heart. He is in my heart. He is in this straw. He is in this pillar also." Prahlada pointed out four places. But why did Lord Narayana come out of the pillar? Because Prahlada had his full concentration with full feeling, "Sarva-bhavena", in the pillar alone. He wished the Lord Hari should come out of the pillar. This was his *Satsankalpa*.

## BHAKTI: THE BEST MEANS

त्रिसत्यस्य भक्तिरेव गरीयसी भक्तिरेव गरीयसी ॥८१॥

**Sutra 81. Trisatyasya bhaktireva gariyasi bhaktireva gariyasi.**

*Only love of the absolute, eternal truth is the greatest; this love indeed, is the greatest.*

त्रिसत्यस्य Trisatyasya: of the absolute, eternal truth; भक्तिः Bhakti: devotion: एव eva: alone; गरीयसि Gariyasi: is greater; भक्तिः Bhakti: devotion; एव eva: only; गरीयसि Gariyasi: is greater.

In all the three periods of time, i.e., past, present and future, devotion alone weighs heaviest (most glorious), devotion alone weighs heaviest (most glorious).

Of the three true paths, the path of devotion is greater than anything else; it is greater than any thing else.

In this Sutra Narada emphasised the value and importance of devotion. Divine love is eternal.

Repetition of the word "Gariyasi" adds force. It glorifies devotion to the highest degree.

Bhakti alone is preferable to other paths, Bhakti alone is preferable.

The path of devotion is the highest path. Love of God is supreme. Devotion to God is devotion to Eternal Truth.

Trisatyam: The three eternal truths are (1) *Jnana*, (2) *Karma* and (3) *Bhakti*. God is love, goodness and truth. God is experienced by the devotee as love. God is experienced by the Karma Yogin as goodness. God is experienced by the Jnani as Truth. Narada says that the first is better than any other.

According to all the three forms of Truth practised through the body, speech and mind, the path of devotion is the best path.

Truth as practised through the body, speech and mind called the three forms of truth. The Holy Rishi Narada has realised the superiority of devotion from the standpoint of all these three Truths.

In the 12th chapter of the Gita, Lord Krishna says, "The devotee is *Yukta Tama*" the best and highest among those who are united to Him.

"Among all Yogis he who, full of faith, with his inner Self merged in Me, worships me, he is deemed by Me to be the most divine." Gita VI. 47. Thus the Bhakta is given the highest place.

Para Bhakti and Jnana are one. Para Bhakti is superior to Mukhya Bhakti even. In Para Bhakti the devotee is one with his higher Self. The object of his love now is not the Personal God but the Absolute. The devotee now passes beyond time, space and causation, beyond the three Gunas, beyond the three states of waking, dream and deep sleep, even beyond the *Triputi* or subject-object relationship. He realises his oneness with the Lord.

गुणमाहात्म्यासक्तिरूपासक्तिपूजासक्तिस्मरणासक्तिदास्यासक्ति
सख्यासक्तिवात्सल्यासक्तिकान्तासक्त्यात्मनिवेदनासक्तितन्मया
सक्तिपरमविरहासक्तिरूपैकधाप्येकादशधा भवति ॥८२॥

**Sutra 82. Gunamahatmyasaktirupasakti pujasakti smaranasakti dasyasakti sakhyasakti vatsalyasakti kantasakti atmanivedanasakti tanmayasakti paramavirahasakti rupaikadhapyekadasadha bhavati.**

*Bhakti or Divine Love, though in itself one only, manifests itself in the following eleven forms: (1) Love of the glorification of the Lord's blessed qualities, (2) Love of his enchanting beauty, (3) Love of worship, (4) Love of constant remembrance, (5) Love of service. (6) Love of Him as a friend. (7) Love of Him as a son or child. (8) Love for Him as that of a wife for her husband, (9) Love of self-surrender to Him, (10) Love of complete absorption in Him, (11) Love of the pain of separation from Him.*

(एकधा Ekadha: of one way, of one kind; अपि Api: Even) गुणमाहात्म्यासक्ति Gunamahatmyasakti: love for glorifying the divine attributes; रूपासक्ति Rupasakti: love of divine beauty; पूजासक्तिः Pujasakti: Love of worship; स्मरणासक्ति smaranasakti: love of remembering; दास्यसक्तिः Dasyasakti: love of service; सख्यसक्तिः Sakhyasakti: Love of God as a friend; वात्सल्यासक्तिः Vatsalyasakti: love of God as that of a child; कान्तासक्तिः Kantasakti: Love of God as that of a wife; आत्मनिवेदनसक्तिः Atmanivedanasakti: love of self-surrender; तन्मयासक्तिः Tanmayasakti love of complete absorption in Him; परमविरहासक्तिः Paramavirahasaktih: love of the pain of separation from Him; रूपासक्तिः Rupa in the form: एकादशधा Ekadasadha: of eleven forms; भवति Bhavati: becomes.

First of all the devotee serves the Lord as a servant serves his master. Then he approaches Him nearer and behaves towards Him as a friend does towards a friend. The relationship is then felt to be more closely personal. Therefore, the devotee rises higher and manifests parental affection for the loved one, as a father for his son. Lastly, the little remaining remoteness between them disappears altogether. The two become one in spirit. The devotee develops all the marks of a beloved wife's love for her beloved husband. In *Atmanivedana* or complete self-surrender, there is complete self-absorption. He feels the living presence of God anywhere and everywhere and permanently loses himself in the Lord.

You can know you love the Lord when you feel you cannot live without Him.

The purpose of the life of a devotee is to lose all sense of distinctive personality and be dissolved in the Lord like camphor in the fire.

Narada and Vyasa, Sukadeva, Kakabhusundi, Sesha, Suta, Saunaka, Sandilya, Bhishma, Prithu, Parikshit and Janamejaya delighted themselves in singing the glories of the Lord. The Gopis of Brindavan, the Rishis of Dandakaranya were naturally attracted by Sri Krishna's enchanting personal beauty. Ambarisha, Lakshmi, Prithu, Bharata spent whole time in worship; Prahlada, Dhruva, Sankara in remembrance; Hanuman, Akrura, Vidura in service. Uddhava, Arjuna, Sudama and Guha had the attribute of friendship; Sridama, Rukmini and Satyabhama loved Sri Krishna as a husband and Dasaratha, Kausalya, Devaki, Nanda, Yasoda, Kasyapa, Aditi, Manu Satarupa, as their son. Bali, Vibhishana, Hanuman, Ambarisha, Sibi did complete self-surrender to the Lord. Sanatkumar, Suka, Sanaka and Yajnavalkya immersed themselves in His Bliss *(Tanmayasakti)*. Uddahava, Arjuna, Gopis and Radha experienced anguish of separation. Each one is characterised by a predominant attitude. All these eleven forms of Bhakti are possible for the same Bhaktas during different moods.

Viraha is the highest manifestation of love. It is a common characteristic of all devotees, because it is in the very nature of intense love that it cannot bear separation. This is one of the supreme tests of devotion in Sutra 29. This stage of love is typically manifested in Radha and the Gopis when they were separated from Sri Krishna.

If all these forms of attachments cannot be developed together, you can select one or two sentiments and cultivate love for God accordingly. Love is fundamentally one. Therefore, no distinction of higher and lower should be made among devotees, according to the difference of sentiment cultivated by them.

All these eleven types of divine love were found developed among the Gopis.

The nine modes or stages of Bhakti are described here. The highest is *Madhurya Rasa* or *Kantasakti* where the lover and the beloved become one. Sufis also entertain this Bhava. The Bhakta begins with *Dasya Bhava*, attitude of a servant like Hanuman. This is the lowest rung in the ladder of Bhakti. Then he takes up a friendly attitude towards God, like Arjuna. Fear vanishes now. He claims equality with his object of worship. Then he develops a Bhava of parental affection towards God. He takes Lord Krishna as his son.

The students of the school of thought of Sri Vallabhacharya Sampradaya entertain this Bhava. All fears and expectations vanish. There is fear of downfall in *Kantasakti*, if the devotee is not careful. He is carried away by lustful propensities. He mistakes physical sensations for devotion. Emotion is not devotion. Many unhappy, unpleasant occurences take place in those who cherish this Bhava. A high standard of purity is required in those who take this Bhava. This Bhava is purely mental. Dressing like a female and showing gestures like a woman is mere hypocritical show. This is not necessary in this Bhava.

# CONCLUSION

इत्येवं वदन्ति जनजल्पनिर्भया एकमताः कुमारव्यास-
शुकशाण्डिल्यगर्गविष्णुकौण्डिल्यशेषोद्धावारुणि
बलिहनूमद्विभीषणादयो भक्ताचार्याः ॥८३॥

**Sutra 83. Ityevam vadanti janajalpanirbhaya ekamatah
kumaravyasasukasandilyagargavishnukoun
dilyaseshoddha varunibalihanumadvibhishanadayo
bhaktacharyah.**

*Thus, the teachers of devotion, Sanatkumara, Vyasa,
Suka, Sandilya, Garga, Vishnu, Koundilya, Sesha, Uddhava,
Aruni, Bali, Hanuman, Vibhishana, etc., proclaim unanimously in this strain, without fear of the carping criticisms
of men.*

इत्येवम् Ityevam: in the manner described above,
जनजल्पनिर्भयाः Jana Jalpa Nirbhaya: fearless of the
prattle of people; एकमताः Ekamatah: of unani-
mous opinion; कुमारव्यासशुकशाण्डिल्यगर्गविष्णुकौण्डिल्यशेषो-
द्धावा-रुणिबलि हनूमद्विभीषणादिः Kumara, Vyasa, Suka,
Sandilya, Garga, Vishnu, Kaundillya, Sesha, Uddhava,
Aruni, Bali, Hanuman, Vibhishana and others; भक्ताचार्याः
Bhaktacharya: teachers of devotion: वदन्ति Vadanti: say,
declare.

The names given above are of the highest personalities in the realm of devotees, who held the same view
as Rishi Narada on this subject.

They are not afraid of being criticised by anyone, because they have the inner conviction of spiritual experience.

Giving the reference of other principal teachers of the path of Bhakti, Narada strengthens his own point of view.

Kumara is Sanatkumara who was the Guru of Narada. He is constantly engaged in the Japa of the Mantra, "Hari Saranam" (Refuge in Sri Hari). He is the prince among Bhaktas. He is one of the pioneers in the path of devotion. Sandilya, the author of Sandilya Sutra, is an Acharya in the path of Bhakti.

Garga is an ancient Rishi. He obtained knowledge of the 64 Vidyas from Siva Himself as a result of penance and worship. He performed the Namakarana ceremony of Sir Krishna. He knew Sri Krishna to be Parabrahman. He is a great authority on astrology. His teaching is recorded as Garga Samhita.

Maharishi Vishnu was a reputed author of Smriti. He was ever absorbed in meditation. Lord Sesha is engaged day and night in singing the praises of Sri Hari through his thousand tongues. He is the teacher of servant-sentiment, *Dasya-Bhava*.

Uddhava was the most intimate friend of Sri Krishna. Bali was the very embodiment of the sentiment of self-surrender. Moved by his devotion, Lord Hari had to undertake the duty of a watchman at his gate. Hanuman is the greatest devotee. He had *Dasya Bhava*. Vibhishana gained the friendship of Lord Rama through Hanuman. All these Acharyas of Bhakti have established the supremacy of Bhakti through the examples of their lives.

This Sutra indicates that Bhakti is a practical method of approaching God which has been adopted with success by a good many devotees placed in different stations in life, that treatise is a compendium of their views written by one

who himself has practised what he preaches and that it is
worth while to follow and profit by the teachings of these
disinterested Masters of Bhakti.

य इदं नारदप्रोक्तं शिवानुशासनं विश्वसति श्रद्धते स
भक्तिमान्भवति स प्रेष्ठं लभते स प्रेष्ठं लभते इति ॥८४॥

**Sutra 84. Ya Idam Naradaproktam sivanusasanam visvasati
sraddhate sa bhaktiman bhavati sa preshtam
labhate sa preshtham labhate iti.**

*He who believes and has faith in this aupsicious teach-
ing expounded by Narada becomes endowed with Bhakti and
realises the most beloved (Lord), attains the most beloved
(Lord).*

यः Ya: who; इदम् Idam: this; नारदप्रोक्तं
Naradaproktam: recited by Narada; शिवानुशासनं
Sivanusasanam: auspicious teaching; विश्वसति Visvasati:
believes; श्रद्धते Shraddhate: practises with faith; सः Sah: he;
भक्तिमान् Bhaktiman: possessed of devotion; भवति Bhavati:
becomes; प्रेष्ठम् Preshtam: the most beloved Lord; लभते
Labhate: realises, obtains; सः Sa: He; प्रेष्ठं Prestham: the
most loved Lord; लभते Labhate: attains; इति Iti: thus.

This is the *Phala Sruti*. What is got is the most beloved
Lord. *Preshtam* is Lover-Husband. It is used here as a
synonym for the highest goal of human life. 'Iti' thus. This
word marks the end of the treatise.

Narada now describes the fruit of devotion. He says
that he who believes, respects and practises these holy
teachings, originally laid down by the first teacher of
Bhakti, Lord Siva, enunciated and elaborated by
Devarishi Narada, attains God in the form of the
"Beloved."

The *Upasamhara* (conclusion) is quite consistent with the *Upakrama* (beginning). There is a beautiful recapitulation of the Sutras, 2, 3, 4, 5 and 6 in this last Sutra.

*Glory to the Lord! Glory to Sage Narada!*

Glory to all Saints, Bhaktas, Bhagavatas and Mahatmas!

Om Tat Sat! Om Santi, Santi, Santi!

# AIMS AND OBJECTS OF
## THE DIVINE LIFE SOCIETY

THE DIVINE LIFE SOCIETY HAS BEEN
ESTABLISHED

*I. To disseminate Spiritual Knowledge*

(a) By publication of books, pamphlets and magazines dealing with ancient, oriental and occidental philosophy and religion in the modern scientific manner, and their distribution on such terms as may appear expedient to the Board of Trustees;

(b) By propagating the Name of the Almighty, and by holding and arranging spiritual discourses and conferences and frequent cultural or spiritual gatherings for the welfare of the humanity:

(c) By establishing training centres or societies for the practice of Yoga, for moral and spiritual Sadhanas and the revival of true culture, to enable aspirants to achieve regeneration through worship, devotion, wisdom, right action and meditation with systematic training in Asanas, Pranayama, Pratyahara, Dharana, Dhyana and

(d) By doing all such acts and things as may be necessary and conducive to the moral, spiritual and cultural uplift of mankind in general and to the attainment of the above-mentioned objects in Bharatavarsha in particular;

## II. To Establish and run Educational Institutions

On modern lines and on right basic principles and to help deserving students by granting them refundable and non-refundable scholarships and also help them for doing research work in the various branches of philosophy and comparative religion, and also to train them to disseminate spiritual knowledge in the most effective manner:

## III. To Help Deserving Orphans and Destitutes

By rendering them such assistance as the Society may deem proper, whether in any individual case or in any particular class of cases;

## IV. To Establish and Run Medical Organisations

Or any other medical institutions and hospitals or dispensaries for the treatment of diseases and dispensing medicines and performing surgical operations, etc., to the poor in particular and to the other public in general, on such terms and in such manner as may be deemed expedient by the Board of Trustees;

## V. To Take Such Other Steps from Time to Time

As may be necessary for effecting a quick and effective moral and spiritual regeneration in the world and in Bharatavarsha in particular.

\* \* \*

*This Society was registered as a Trust in the year 1936 and has been actively functioning since then to fulfil the above sublime aims and objects in the world.*